ORBITAL MANAGEMENT:
Beyond the Hierarchy

By:

Jay H. Lehr
Executive Director
National Water Well Association
Dublin, Ohio

and

Jose E. Rodriguez
J. Ensor Enterprises, Inc.
Xenia, Ohio

Hamilton Press
Abt Books

British Cataloging in Publication Information Available

Co-published by arrangement with Abt Books.

Library of Congress Cataloging-in-Publication Data

Lehr, Jay H., 1936-
  Orbital management.

  Includes index.
  1. Decentralization in management. I. Rodriguez,
Jose E., 1958-   . II. Title.
HD50.L44   1987   658.4'02   87-143
  ISBN 0-8191-6264-7 (alk. paper)
  ISBN 0-8191-6265-5 (pbk. : alk. paper)

All Hamilton Press books are produced on acid-free
paper which exceeds the minimum standards set by the National
Historical Publication and Records Commission.

Acknowledgements

SPECIAL APPRECIATION IS DUE TO PAM BELL for continued assistance and support in preparing and revising this manuscript as it evolved over the years, to the staff of the National Water Well Association which willingly served as a living model of an innovative management system, and finally, to the countless men and women we have encountered in various organizations over the years who have shared their likes and dislikes of the organizations in which they have served.

Jay H. Lehr
Jose E. Rodriguez
July 1986

Contents

PREFACE   xi

FOREWORD: ABOUT THE IDEAS AND THE
AUTHORS   xiii

A NOTE ON GENDER   xvi

Chapter 1.   ORBITAL MANAGEMENT SYSTEMS:
             AN INTRODUCTION   1
             A creative step beyond the hierarchy

Chapter 2.   DEFINING THE MANAGEMENT
             ROLES   14
             Management roles in an orbital system
             tend to be somewhat amorphous and over-
             lapping yet boundaries and responsibility
             levels are definable for department heads,
             division managers and group leaders.

Chapter 3.   PLANNING AND DECISION-MAKING
             IN OPEN ORBIT   17
             In any organization, planning at some op-
             timum level and scope is critical to success.
             The level and scope within an orbital sys-
             tem is significantly different from that of a
             hierarchy.
             Concurrently all managers develop a style
             for decision-making which can at times be
             quite idiosyncratic rather than pragmatic.
             Whatever the method, it is essentially out
             in the open for all to see within an orbital
             system.

Chapter 4.   EFFICIENCY VS. CREATIVITY   23

All systems strive toward efficiency, though many fail. Some systems promote creativity and most fail. There are considerable conflicts between these two objectives if desired simultaneously. The orbital system allows an interesting solution to this managerial problem.

Chapter 5.   MEETINGS: WHEN, WHERE, WHY?   26

The majority of managers classify meetings as their primary time-waster. Meetings do have their place and the orbital system dictates their efficient and productive utilization in a naturally selective manner.

Chapter 6.   STAFFING UP AND BREAKING IN   29

When do we need additional people and how do we find and select them? The answers to these questions are less obvious in the orbital system and require a higher degree of scrutiny.

When new people are added their optimum acclimation lies somewhere between the Welcome-Wagon and a fraternity initiation.

Chapter 7.   CREATING YOUR OWN JOB WHILE
             TRAVELING IN ORBIT   35

An objective devoutly to be wished, but rarely achieved. Orbital management not only establishes the possibility, but in fact makes it a virtual requirement.

Movement within a single orbit as well as from orbit to orbit is nearly without obstacle, and results in a freedom of spirit which breaks the stereotyped bounds of the working world.

Chapter 8.   CLERKS AND TYPISTS NO MORE   41

The orbital system offers an exceptionally high level of self-determination in the fulfillment of various functions and tasks;

individuals cease to feel like warm-blooded machines. Titles then become obsolete.

Functional hierarchical classifications frequently carry negative connotations that create self-fulfilling mind sets which stifle productivity and growth. It may seem to be more form than substance but these negative descriptors must be expunged from common use.

Some Chief Operating Officers could even function without a titled secretary, in the Orbital System.

Chapter 9. ABSENTEEISM, SICK LEAVE AND
            THE WORKING DAY: A NEW LOOK
            AT OLD PROCEDURES   50

In a reasonably successful orbital system, a variety of refreshing and beneficial personnel practices can be instituted which will minimize necessary sick leave, all but eliminate absenteeism, and maximize employee enthusiasm.

Chapter 10. ADVANCEMENT ON MERIT   55

A case is made for advancement by natural selection which has potential for eliminating the debilitating effects of Dr. Peter's principle.

The air of equality which permeates the orbital system results in an unusual competition between the self-made employee and those who are college educated.

Chapter 11. NEPOTISM: A NEW LOOK   61

The orbital management system not only proves that nepotism (long considered a taboo) is workable, but in fact makes a strong case for its active development within a corporate structure.

Chapter 12. MAKING WORK FUN   64

Making work fun may sound like a sophomoric objective, but through careful devel-

opment of pleasing activities the sharp line
between work and play can be turned into
a smooth transition.

Similarly a warm and open atmosphere
and concern for aesthetics in the physical
office environment are important features
of orbital office layouts.

Chapter 13. LONELINESS AND THE PAYMASTER   69

When only one staff member carries the
weight of knowledge about each employee's salary, he needs special personality
characteristics to cope with the peer pressures.

Chapter 14. THE TEMPORARY NEED FOR
MARTIAL LAW   72

Even in the highly developed democratic
system of orbital management, periodic
episodes of crisis may require that social
niceties be temporarily relinquished in favor of rapid-fire, military-style response.

Chapter 15. ABUSE   75

Given enough rope some people will hang
themselves. Given enough freedom in the
orbital system, from time to time some
people will abuse it.

Chapter 16. THE BOARD OF DIRECTORS . . . A
NECESSARY EVIL   78

Hiring and firing the COO may prove to
be a Board's only saving grace.

Chapter 17. REFLECTIONS OF COMPANY IMAGE   81

Organizations tend to develop an image of
themselves which may be far removed
from reality. Periodic inspection and reflection is a must to minimize that erosive
hypocrisy.

Chapter 18. A CLOSE BRUSH WITH THEORY   84

Management theory is replete with obtuse
pomposity full of sound and fury signify-
ing little. But a little sense of whence we
came is worth the effort.

Chapter 19. CRITICAL MASS   88

No system of management will be optimally effective for a wide range of corporate sizes. Orbital management is most
effective in its own distinct range. Happily
most companies fall within that range, but
when size exceeds management's control
two orbital systems under one corporate
structure may prove superior to a single
hierarchy.

Chapter 20. ORBITAL MANAGEMENT AS A
SOLUTION   95

An orbital management system certainly is
not a panacea for all organizational situations, but it does provide a new approach
for those organizations concerned with
productivity, flexibility and employee relations.

Chapter 21. AND NOW FOR THE BAD NEWS . . .   97

A penetrating analysis of all the negative
criticism which can be realistically aimed at
the innovative orbital system.

INDEX   101

Preface

THE PURPOSE OF THIS BOOK is to introduce an innovative and comprehensive management concept. Orbital management is aimed at building a decentralized structure, either as an entire system or as a partial entity within other forms of management structures such as hierarchies. We address not only the structural aspect of an orbital system but also the behavioral and organizational functions of such a system. Once established, an orbital system can reward management through its flexibility in addressing both the internal and external environments of an organization, the creativity and productivity of self-managed employees, and the self-perpetuation of this organic and humanistic approach to management.

It is our aim to show the reader that orbital systems, large or small, can be built successfully and in fact do exist. We do not attempt to identify the exact steps needed to build a system. We simply introduce the concept in form. It would be a difficult task to show the many methodologies and industries in which orbital systems may be introduced and applied. We have purposely avoided identification with specific firms in order not to prejudice the reader to a particular size of an organization. Orbital management principles may be applied to a variety of industries and circumstances. It is more important for the reader to absorb the form of the concept and later shape the substance to his or her unique situation.

Many of the principles inherent to orbital management were theoretically introduced many years ago as Theory Y, participative management, the decentralization concept and, more recently, the Japanese management style. If American business managers want to understand and communicate with their markets, increase the productivity of their employees, and react quickly to their internal and external environments, then they must be able to divorce themselves from the rigid trappings of the many hierarchical structures which they have created. The first step in building an orbital system begins with a total commitment by management and a focus on individuals within their organizations. No matter how large or small one's organization may be, orbital management principles may be established successfully either on a partial basis or as a whole system. Communication is an underlying premise of orbital management. An orbital system provides a vehicle to facilitate communication, internally or externally.

We hope that the reader will not only be able to absorb the form of the orbital management concept but also take the opportunity to apply it, if not wholly, at least to an effective extent.

Foreword:

About the Ideas and the Authors

THIS BOOK GREW OUT OF THE COMBINED MANAGE-
MENT STYLES AND IDEOLOGIES OF THE AUTHORS.
When they first met about six years ago, they had developed
separate but similar approaches to management practices—Lehr
through practice and Rodriguez through research and consult-
ing.

Shared ideas on management drew them closer together. Over
the years, the National Water Well Association, where Lehr is
Executive Director, had received many requests for guidance and
advice on how different aspects of the orbital management system
could be utilized in other companies. About eight years ago, Lehr
asked publishers about the possibility of codifying the orbital
management program in a popular book, and was told that those
theories were perhaps too heretical and that the business community would not be open to such innovation. Happily, time has
marched forward and their views are no longer considered as
heretical as they once were. Together they decided to give birth to
a concise, easily-readable manuscript that would explain the
hows, whats, and whys of this refreshing system for others to
assimilate into their organizations if they were so inclined.

Jay Lehr had prepared himself for a life of teaching, research and writing on a college campus, the kind of life he saw as unfettered by the rigidities of bureaucracy and as fostering necessary creative freedom. When academic life proved to be closer to that reflected in Edward Albee's play, "Who's Afraid of Virginia Wolff," Lehr left Ohio State University in 1967 to take over the National Water Well Association, a fledgling professional society and trade association which seemed willing to be led in any number of productive directions. He was its first full-time staff member.

Jose Rodriguez came to the Midwest from the Washington, D.C. area. He spent both his undergraduate and graduate years researching different management concepts and entrepreneurial practices, and had noticed that many organizations—through their managers and through management practices—stifled the creativity and the quality of work produced by employees. He had separately reached the same conclusions and developed the same aspirations as Lehr: that every organization—whether a service or manufacturing company—should *and could* build and maintain a working environment conducive to high productivity and employee satisfaction, with quality workmanship the essential by-product. Rodriguez' scholarly background in business management made it possible to insure that this book focused on the unique aspects of orbital management that more hierarchical systems commonly lack.

From the beginning at the National Water Well Association, Lehr assumed that the work lifestyle he wanted would appeal to fellow workers, although such a style had always been thought unobtainable. As the organization grew, every effort was made to hire people who wanted independence and freedom in exchange for unusually high productivity. Experimenting with different management concepts, he successfully derived the Orbital Management concept, and began the creation of a manual that would explain in detail to Association staff the intricacies of the system under which they were operating. These ideas were initially met with skepticism from the business world, and Lehr was viewed as something of an iconoclast and a heretic.

Today the National Water Well Association has a staff of more than 70, and its beautiful new office facility has become the center of research, education and publishing for ground-water science throughout the world. Hundreds of people visit the Association each year and experience the refreshing and dynamic atmosphere evident on a walk through the Headquarters building.

Since these ideas first began to take shape on paper, and during joint efforts by the authors to refine the orbital concept, other innovative individuals and companies began using more humanistic approaches within their organizations. Companies like Apple Computer were founded and developed on similar free-wheeling approaches, although the record shows clearly that size often alters the earlier, loosely-structured personalities of the smaller and perhaps more successful companies. William Gore of Gore, Inc. applied an equally free spirit that made Goretex a household word among runners and outdoorsmen, who can now weather the rain and cold without concern. Gore still retains the refreshing management concepts that allow a successful company to hire good men, let them run loose to find a job, create their own titles, and add exponentially to the productivity of the corporate structure. Don Burr of Peoples Express Airlines introduced a new management style to an ailing airline industry and exploded that organization into one of the most successful entrepreneurial ventures of the decade. (The more recent decline of Peoples is likely a result of size outdistancing the management style.)

The Japanese management technique, once the wonder of the Western world, is now widely accepted as a concept applicable here in the United States and abroad. It is perhaps the Japanese whose managerial skills (although not fully applicable in the United States for cultural reasons) are most responsible for opening the minds of American businessmen to alternate approaches for dealing with their employees and maximizing employee productivity.

The reader will find all of the ideas in this book refreshing, most of them new, many already put into place elsewhere. But the greatest value may be the definitive manner in which the authors describe how this same matrix of management techniques can be readily implemented elsewhere in the business world.

A Note on Gender

Any words such as he, his, him or himself which may be perceived as describing only the male of the species in fact refer to men and women interchangeably. Use of such words is simply for ease of reading.

Originally, the book included reference to both genders. Our editor found the text to be awkward, and we felt compelled to follow her advice.

Chapter 1 /

Orbital Management Systems: An Introduction

Historical Perspective

IN THE WORLD OF BUSINESS MANAGEMENT, a hierarchy is defined by Webster's Third Edition as "a group of persons arranged in successive orders or classes each of which is subject to or dependent on the one above it." A less sophisticated, though perhaps more practical, terminology would be the "pecking order." The vast majority of all organizations known to man function under such an arrangement and, we hope to illustrate, frequently malfunction because of it. At the very least, organizations fail to obtain the full potential of the working group both in personal productivity and job satisfaction. The net result is a less than efficient organization.

It is probable that present day refinements of organizational theory stretch back through recorded time to military operations,[1] when the need for structure came as quickly as the need for self-defense. As military history is the best recorded facet of man's evolution and development, its organizational or management structure is exceedingly well documented.

When the industrial revolution advanced business and manufacturing past the level of cottage industry, local craftsmen, and traders, the need for organization and management concepts developed whcrc no serious need or problem existed before.

The obvious similarities in directing an army and directing a team of factory workers did not escape early managers. From this knowledge the standard hierarchy which ultimately launched today's prevailing management systems developed. Slave labor is gone, sweat shops are few and unions have effectively eliminated most unfair labor practices, but certainly no real alteration in the initial military structure has occurred. Personnel rank—be it captain, lieutenant, sergeant, or private; plant manager, shop foreman, assembly line chief, or lathe operator; vice president, department head, administrative assistant, or clerk—means that each person is inferior to those above him in the hierarchy and superior to those below. As a result, each person must take orders from above while having an opportunity to give orders to those below.

The system is not without its advantages as it offers the opportunity for rapid activity in the face of crisis (such as a military battle). When necessary, orders can be barked down the line with blind obedience expected and normally obtained. It also offers security to individuals as their place in the scheme of the organization is clear and unambiguous. That is to say Mr. "D" answers to Ms. "C" and directs Mr. "E." Additionally, it makes clear where future growth and success (or perhaps maintenance of the status quo) can lead one. Likewise, excessive failure (not passivity) will point one in the opposite direction.

The hierarchical system of management is an easy one to establish and maintain. There are few recorded instances of mutiny in the military, and nearly anyone can be placed into the system without a significant need for screening or quality control. It does however require a large number of individuals who do no useful work, but instead police others or duplicate effort. Clearly the use of significant numbers of staff personnel as sergeants or supervisors is indicative of a loss of productivity and thus efficiency, in a perfect world where two plus two would equal four. We believe it is even more destructive of efficiency when one considers the less obvious stifling of human creativity and the natural desire to be free.

It can of course be argued that large groups of people cannot possibly function without extensive supervision, without clear and unambiguous directions and procedures. Further, it must be said that the instinct to be free is not in fact inherent in all mankind, else we would not be so easily restricted in our daily lives.

We will not debate these arguments here. We are able and willing to do so, but it would serve no purpose in this description of a new and more effective concept of "management" we choose to label "orbital." We take this seemingly non-combative course because it is not necessary to prove that this new system is a panacea for all organizations. It need not work under all circumstances, or for all people. Its efficiency need only be proved under certain circumstances and with particular people. Given these conditions it proves to be a clearly superior form of management. That the circumstances for success are reasonably easy to attain is hopefully a conclusion the reader will reach of his or her own accord.

The Orbital System

First, let us explain what orbital management is not.

It is not a hierarchy in which everyone is placed on a vertical ladder. It is not a system where the path of advancement is either automatic or even obvious. It is not an organization where the existence of a boss-employee relationship is apparent. It is not a structure made heavy and inflexible by an abundance of explicit rules, regulations or procedures. It is not a format under which one can expect to perform a set list of tasks or pattern of functions and be highly praised for doing one's part. It does not reward mediocrity. It does not stifle creativity. It does not tell one when to pass "GO" and when to "proceed directly to jail." It is not for all people.

Orbital management is in fact a horizontal, single-plane structure where essentially equal levels of responsibility rotate around higher levels of responsibility. All levels are at once dependent on the rotational center, independent in its own operation and interdependent upon all other orbiting units. It works much like the solar system in which the earth rotates around the sun, gaining energy from it but simultaneously spinning independently on its own axis and working in concert with other bodies in the solar system.

At this point, one picture or diagram will be worth any number of words in understanding the concept. Figure 1 illustrates a business organization's orbital management system.

The center of any orbital organization is the chief operating officer (COO or CO_2)[2]; his is the same position that would occupy

Figure 1. Orbital Management
          Organization Structure

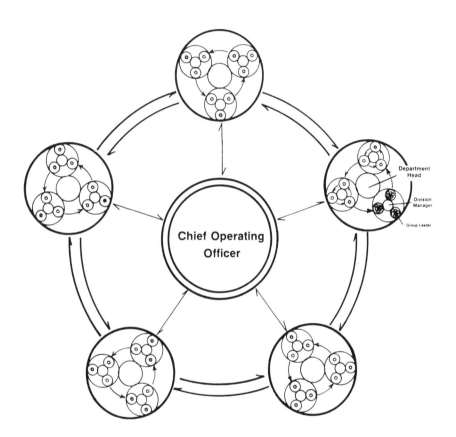

the top of a hierarchical pyramid. Here the resemblance between the hierarchical and orbital management system ends.

In the orbital system, the chief operating officer is less the godlike leader of the hierarchy and more an individual who is responsible for keeping the solar system turning. The COO essentially furnishes lubrication to the spheres that rotate around his office in the form of departments, functioning not unlike a ballbearing. The COO is the hub of the bearing; the departments are the balls in the ring rotating around the hub.

Each departmental sphere[3] rotates on its own axis while turning around the hub in which the COO resides and each departmental sphere has a hub occupied by the department head, around which turn the spheres we shall call divisions. These again have independent rotation in addition to their movement around the department head. Divisional spheres have as their hub a Division Manager who may have independent units rotating about him or her. These are called groups and rotate again on their own axis around a hub representing the Group Leader. In the model shown in the figure only staff is shown beyond the group leader, though further orbiting levels could obviously be developed if the size of the organization required it.

One of the more interesting innovations in the orbiting concept is that it allows an individual to wear more than one hat. He could be the hub in one rotating sphere and a ball in the bearing of another. In terms of hierarchical structure this would mean being an indian in one group and a chief in another, an improbable situation. But orbital management relies neither on indians nor chiefs, but rather on cooperating flexible individuals not significantly aware of rank, but instead stationed within the system in accordance with variations in responsibility. These responsibility levels are clear and unambiguous, eliminating any genuine possibility for a lack of appreciation or respect between orbit levels or obvious salary differentials. Salary is determined according to responsibility, skill, training, seniority and other standard measures common to other systems. It is not normally known among the staff how other staff members are salaried.

There is no special limit on the number of departments that rotate around the chief operating officer, the number of divisions which rotate around a department head, or the number of groups that rotate around a division manager. This will depend on the ability of the hub individual to adequately provide the lubrication to keep the balls in his bearing rotating efficiently, as well as on the desire, need or potential for a sphere in the bearing to move into a higher rotational orbit. Decisions in the direction of this type of growth are determined as a result of orderly evolution rather than artificial reordering.

Thus a possibility exists for advancement by any level of staff, but advancement to a further degree of rotational ring is not guaranteed or assured. A staff member may become a group leader, a group leader may become a division manager, and a divison manager may become a department head, but there is no assurance that it will happen. Since there is only room for one chief operating officer, a department head would only advance to that position if the COO left the organization. By the same method, it is possible for a group leader or division manager to advance to a further level of rotation by taking the position of a person who has left, thus leaving his own rotating unit behind in lower orbit.

It should be obvious that when a rotating unit advances in orbit, it results in the advancement of all managerial personnel in the unit.

Planning for Future Leadership

Returning for a moment to the departmental orbit, it is important or at least useful in the system to feel that more than one of the department heads is both willing and able to advance to the position of chief operating officer if the COO left. This is so because the democratic equality of co-workers on which the system depends operates best when advancement is from inside the organization rather than outside. At the same time it is equally important that no department head be delegated first among equals or heir apparent. This frustrates the freedom and equality of the system and ultimately stifles the creative growth of all units in the orbit.

We cannot overemphasize how important it is not to differentiate among personnel serving as focal points or hubs of units rotating on the same orbit. A breakdown in the coexistent mutuality leads to the development of unofficial hierarchical pecking orders, breeds distrust in the system's integrity, and results in the eventual demise of its special productivity. Continual reinforcement of the system is of crucial importance, and this is done through practical work situations which utilize the interaction of managerial groups exercising equal jurisdictional impact on the establishment of policy or production-oriented decisions. Not to do this leads to a system exhibiting form but not substance. It should be further emphasized that outside influences not be allowed to create differential power or authority in the organization—this too can be divisive. Positive reinforcement between managerial personnel can and should effectively nullify such uncontrollable outside influence.

Orbital Succession

Similar development of qualified successors should occur in each orbital unit to make advancement from within possible, just as it is in a conventional hierarchical system. This will not always be practical, particularly where rapid horizontal growth within a unit requires addition of high-level people with new skills or simply more people with old skills than can be supplied from outer orbiting groups. The development of potential internal orbital succession is a plan which should always be subscribed to and worked toward, even though it may not exist at a given point in time.

Systematic Equality

The concept of equality of orbiting units is the strength and backbone of the orbital management system.

Within each orbit of departments, divisions and groups there are absolutely no hierarchical relationships between heads, managers or leaders. All are autonomous in their departments, divisions or groups and are completely equal with other heads, managers and leaders. Similarly the hub around which their group rotates does not play a commanding role but, as mentioned previously, takes a lubricating role. This role is one of leadership by example, participation, support and cooperation. There is no pulling of rank, no fighting over turf. It is easy at this point to assume such organizational relationships to be unrealistic and beyond the realm of adaptive human behavior, but this is not so. For it to work simply requires positive reinforcement among and between the members of the group, beginning with the chief operating officer who must convince each outer orbit of the sincerity and feasibility of the system. It requires a near total separation from past experience in the outside world of management. In essence the chief operating officer is viewed not as the big boss with terminal power over all employees, but rather as an individual whose job it is to keep the system turning as productively and creatively as possible. That may include helping any department as needed by offering new ideas, being the sounding board for others, coordinating interdependency among the departments and insuring the independence of each unit.

To illustrate this point more completely, the orbital system could even allow the chief operating officer to drop back into the departmental orbit as a department head without feeling demoted. Both positions are well defined and autonomous, with nearly equal opportunities to exercise independent creativity as the head of a company, organization or unit.

Upward Mobility

In the departmental orbit each unit or department is essentially an independent business operation with an autonomous entrepreneurial department head functioning as the president of his or her own company. While the department head has no realistic upward mobility, there is no need for any because there are no limitations on the potential growth of the department or the department head. The individual is already top dog in his or her own organization with no overbearing superior influence to produce a drive for greater independence.

It soon becomes evident that the department head has the best of both worlds, with a combination of satisfaction from creative freedom and independence and the supportive security of interdependent assistance from colleagues in and beyond his own orbit. Furthermore, the grinding stultifying obstacles of government regulations and paperwork which wear down many a true entrepreneur do not exist for the department head. These tasks are handled elsewhere in the organization by people better trained and mentally prepared to handle such frustration. Such assistance, for example, comes from the accounting division which normally handles tax, audit, wage and employment regulations, or the publications department which publishes written communications. These people are doing what they enjoy and are trained to do, while taking difficult burdens from the shoulders of others.

A similar independence exists at the divisional level, where again a share of creative freedom exists for each manager who is given a much greater opportunity to develop both technical skill and management talent than is generally possible in a hierarchical organization. Managers have an opportunity to advance that depends more on themselves than on the system itself. If growth in their division leads to increased responsibility and resultant benefit to the company, the prospects of jumping to the inner departmental orbit exist. Such a jump in responsibility level is not easily achieved, but the real existence of such potential produces a driving force in the division manager not commonly found in middle management personnel within a hierarchy.

And so it goes, down to the group leader level and the staff personnel in each group. True democratic equality pervades the system and makes believers out of doubters.

Discipline

Another major advantage is that the orbital management system becomes self-policing and thus self-perpetuating. As individuals in each orbit grow to appreciate the benefits of the organization, they become protective of it. Clearly its success depends on self-starters—motivated individuals who need little supervision. On the other hand, in such an atmosphere it can be a simple matter to goof off and get an apparently free ride. Individuals who do this stick out as running counter to the value system and are quickly ostracized by their peers. More often than not peer pressure will cause their termination before the person in the hub of their sphere would be inclined to take action. Freedom to apply oneself in a responsible manner is an intoxicating atmosphere in which to work. Once gained it is not easily given up; thus participants in the system will work independently to protect it.

Hiring

Some interesting observations can be made here regarding the way in which different individuals react to the "orbital management system." Young people joining such a program right out of high school or college with no other job experience tend not to appreciate it, because they have no frame of referencing the inherent faults that exist elsewhere in more conventional hierarchical systems. The response of these individuals is unpredictable. Special effort must be made to indoctrinate them to appreciate and use their freedom from intense supervision. This will be less important for those with other work experience. It is especially unfortunate when an individual fails to make the grade in an orbital management system, because later adjustment to a hierarchical position is likely to be difficult.

Conversely, individuals too strongly indoctrinated into a hierarchical system of well-defined structure simply do not adapt when allowed exceptional personal discretion in the conduct of their daily work.

An orbitally-managed organization is a haven in which the self-disciplined, self-reliant, and self-motivated thrive. Automatons who must be "plugged in" at 9:00 a.m. and "unplugged" at 5:00 p.m. may enter the system for relatively brief periods, but do not normally remain. Their incapacity for self-growth hinders them from significantly contributing to the organization.

Particular effort is necessary in screening potential candidates for positions in an orbital management system to minimize the risk of failure. An extremely effective method of screening candidates is to establish a search committee for each job opening, made up of individuals who will be co-workers with the new employee and including the hub individual (department head, division manager, or group leader). For this reason orbital management groups can function well without a personnel manager or personnel department as it is best for each rotating sphere to handle its hiring practice independently. Care must be taken in selecting co-workers for a screening committee. They must be secure and highly capable employees, as less substantial persons tend to oppose the selection of more capable individuals. In any case, final decision should rest with the department head or division manager but considerable weight should be given to co-workers' opinions if the exercise is not to be considered a sham.

Opportunity for employees to have a voice in the selection of additional or replacement co-workers also proves to be a significant benefit of the system. It adds to the high level of loyalty and dedication each employee develops toward the company and the system. More obviously, it contributes to a very cohesive and properly integrated rotational unit which tends to develop a personality of its own with an unusual "esprit de corps."

Supervision

Throughout this chapter, we have emphasized the reduced role of supervision in each rotating unit, be it department, division or group. Let us now concentrate on exactly what this means.

The orbital system requires leadership by example. We have said earlier that there are no shop foremen, no full time supervisors. The general rule is that supervisory personnel spend eighty percent of their time doing their own productive work and twenty percent of their time supervising and assisting others. This of course varies from week to week, but the result is that a sense of independence develops in all workers. Every individual prides himself on what he produces, not only on what subordinates produce under his direction.

This scheme places a very heavy burden on supervisors or hub individuals, but the result is worth the effort. These people are only part-time administrators but they are full-time producers. Their work stands on its own merit. Such a system engenders tremendous respect among employees for one another. Hub personnel recognize the ability of their staff to function independently and, in turn, staff members recognize the tremendous work required of their supervisors in addition to the major responsibility for all work performed. Clearly the de-emphasis of supervision is a major constructive feature of orbital management.[4]

Cross-Fertilization

The orbital management system tends to create peer relationships at and across all rotational rings. It further allows what we earlier described as the ability of individuals to wear more than one hat; to serve in the hub of one unit and in the bearing ring of another. This is a result of a frequent desire of individuals to make a contribution in a variety of areas of an organization, or a need for common talent in different departments, divisions or groups. An individual who serves in the hub of one department may wish to make a contribution in another department where he would serve as a division manager, group leader or simply on the staff during the fulfillment of certain tasks.[5]

The chief operating officer may also serve in such a dual capacity where he plays a truly subordinate role to other supervisory personnel in the orbital system. Such role change is exhilarating for the individual, and fully reinforces the sincerity of a system which treats all members of the organization as equal contributors in accordance with their skill, ability, and capacity to serve.

In succeeding chapters we shall describe in detail how various aspects of business management operate and are impacted by the orbital system. Our descriptions are not theoretical but are in fact empirical observations of the management system in operation. We have experimented with this system over the past twelve years, and have personally attempted to develop a work environment so satisfying as to be an extension of one's family life in which personal goals and objectives exist uniquely on an individual level.

An element of utopian thinking clearly exists in our observations; many may identify it as unrealistic polyandry. This may be a fair critique or condemnation at times, but more often the discourse can be justified for its potential as self-fulfilling prophecy. A positive attitude is after all central to the success of the orbital system. In any case, whatever position is taken by the reader, a strong argument can be made for the partial success of an orbital system. Even if we were to admit that total attainment of an orbital system can rarely be achieved (and we are not willing to make that admission), it should become evident to the reader that any significant development of orbit characteristics is superior to a totally hierarchical arrangement.[6]

To work toward the full attainment of an orbital system one should have positive results in almost all cases, thus making it a goal worth working toward even if one is not optimistic regarding its total achievement.

NOTES

1. Historically, the church was also a forefather to our bureaucratic organizations.

2. CO_2 for those chief operating officers who expel hot air.

3. Or profit center

4. A sad organizational example of this occurred in Chinese and American prison camps during the Korean War. The Americans required a one-to-one relationship between guards and prisoners; 600 prisoners, 600 guards. The Chinese in one particular prison camp held 600 prisoners with only two guards, leaving an extra 598 soldiers to engage us in battle.

5. In Lehr's organization, the head of research might at times work under the director of education. The director of publications might choose to serve in some function under the convention director or simply may be needed to do so. This cross-fertilization provides for greater efficiency; the best ideas are freely shared and the entire company benefits.

6. A theory Y organization, in whole or in part, is superior to a theory X organization. See Chapter 18.

Chapter 2 /

Defining the Management Roles

IT CAN BE SAID THAT ONE OBJECTIVE OF ORBITAL MANAGEMENT is to make every employee a manager. If in fact we direct ourselves by defining the form, if not the entire substance, of our work, we are indeed managing ourselves. At the very least this should be the case for every individual in the system. Upon this base we build the management levels of group leader, division manager, department head and chief operating officer.

The separation of their management level is at once both clear and indistinct. It is indistinct in the broad perspective, where we see them all as autonomous entities engaging in a very special task or area of effort.

The separation becomes clear however when one looks closely at both the nature of responsibility resting on the manager and the complexity of the work overseen and performed by a manager. While all managers should be very nearly equally autonomous, the orbit of that autonomy is distinctly further from the system's center of rotation—that is, the department head orbit.

14

Thus a group leader will oversee generally less complex tasks than a division manager and a division manager will be responsible for less critical work than a department head. Parallel to this management variation will be the physical numbers of employees which rotate around each manager. In a later chapter we will discuss optimum numbers involved in the orbital system but, briefly, the number of individuals managed decreases as the orbit's distance from system center (COO) increases. A COO will not normally manage more than seven departments; a department head will not manage more than five divisions; a division manager will not manage more than three groups; a group leader will direct only two employees as a general rule.

While these numbers are not carved in stone, they do indicate the prescribed levels of responsibility. These variations in managerial load should be carefully planned. All staff members must recognize that the orbital variations are designed in a meaningful way rather than being arbitrary or capricious. Similarly, the actual work load at each successive management orbit should increase to show that obvious variations in salary (assumed, not known) will be supported by both the magnitude of effort as well as responsibility.

Respect and recognition of all managers by individuals rotating around them is crucial to the effectiveness of the system because it eliminates internal back-biting or dissension. In addition, it must be possible for staff members to believe that ascension to a high level of management is possible on merit.

Again, the apparent equality of management personnel, and thus the lack of apparent distinction, must be recognized as an important aspect of the system.

Each manager must foster the autonomous system around his individual hub in a manner that will yield thoughtful decisions and fair judgments.

There will obviously be a tendency for cliques to develop among department heads, division managers and group leaders as they represent higher levels of responsibility. This may be valuable if it serves to produce cross-fertilization of management ideas and subsequent personal and company growth. At the same time, no rigid lines should form between the management levels or a group pecking order might result. Such a pecking order is often obscured because individuals frequently hold positions at varying responsibility levels in different orbital units. Thus little is done or discussed behind "closed doors" and a very open communication without barriers is retained. While we consider it self-effacing not to feel more important than others, the system supports such equality. But for the bricklayer, the architect's skill would go unnoticed.

The orbital system thrives on an absence of territorial imperative or turf battles within an orbit of responsibility. It is truly beneficial to make everyone in a management unit capable of replacing everyone else. Each manager should encourage those in orbit around him to covet his own position at the center of the orbit or enable them to jump orbits into an equivalent management level.

This is easier said than done, human nature being what it is, but the orbital system does breed cooperation while minimizing petty jealousies, and enables these uncommon associations.

Chapter 3 /

Planning and Decision-Making in Open Orbit

Planning in Orbit

PLANNERS IN SOME CIRCLES HAVE fallen to a level of respect given the old used car salesman—a result of the planning so much in vogue a decade ago. When the highly touted benefits of planning were not realized and vast sums of money were wasted in all types of organizations (particularly the government), the concept of planning fell on hard times. Most business managers, however, are wise enough not to discard the good with the bad, and recognize that long-range and short-range planning remain an important function of successful business management.

Negative aspects of planning include spending so much time planning that there isn't time to act, or spending so much on planning that money to implement the plan is lacking. Perhaps the most negative aspect involves planning so totally that flexibility or room to fly by the seat of one's pants is eliminated. One must be able to take advantage of opportunities when they occur and not be so restricted by plan as to be forced to let these opportunities go by.

A spontaneity exists in orbital management systems which creates a momentum against highly structured planning. Each managerial unit—rotating on its own axis, developing its own energy, and fueled by its own creativity—tends to grow in a very natural manner without specific planning. People in the system, by their nature, are able to make day-to-day decisions by sizing up all controlling factors. One could, in fact, make an argument against planning because of the restrictive damper it can put on people's enthusiasm. It would be a mistake, however, to accept that argument because, while the role of planning in an orbital system may be less rigid and perhaps even less necessary, it is clearly required for the orbital system to reach optimum output and efficiency.

What is most important in the orbital plan, however, is general direction rather than specific delineation. That is to say, we must anticipate how a managerial unit will develop, but can admit to uncertainty about the actual degree of development. The degree of development will depend on a number of factors and they must be well defined by the orbital manager.

Clearly, without recognition of a need for additional employees, one will not be able to anticipate the need for additional space; without anticipation of increased sales, one cannot anticipate the need for increased production. So planning or forecasting is critical. Where orbital management varies, however, from normal planning is in an emphasis on alternate possibilities in each segment of a plan. The orbital management plan will prepare a manager for a wide variety of mid-course corrections, ensuring that good opportunities need not be passed by nor all decisions be made so quickly as to preclude ample time for consideration. Thus orbital planning focuses on flexible opportunities within a general growth direction. The manager does not carve his future in stone, but instead outlines the directions it may take and some thoughtful responses that would be productive if various situations arise in the future. This type of flexibility is required for all staff members within a rotational unit who are creatively spinning on their own axes. If they are highly constrained by a firm plan, they will not believe in the autonomy of the system and their own creativity will be severely restricted.

It is critical in orbital planning to allow all individuals within a rotational unit the opportunity to participate in the planning function. It is unwise for a department head to plan for his division manager or for division managers to plan for their group leaders.

The first draft of a program plan should be a collective effort. It will obviously be choppy and lacking in cohesion and compatibility, but such structural problems can be easily ironed out in a second stage of group interaction where the plan parts will be molded into a coherent program capable of sustaining the primary objectives of the entire organizational unit. This planning participation is as important or even more important for the word processing operator and mail room clerk as it is for the computer service manager or business manager. Theoretically, the lower one sees oneself on the managerial totem pole the more important it is to recognize the reality of being able to plan one's future output and define personal objectives.

Production of alternate plans for predictable variations in future development is time consuming, but allows for rapid decision making based on previous comprehensive considerations of future developments. Alternate plans tend to minimize crisis-type action/reaction scenarios.

There is no need for planning to become time consuming, laborious, unrealistic and frustrating. Planning at all times should be a futuristic snapshot of where an organizational unit can expect to be, based on where the unit lies presently and in which direction it should go. A five-year plan is best, because it is long enough to require broad flexible thinking yet short enough to have precise milestones established along the way. Once a five-year plan is developed, staff members will find it exciting and productive to update the plan annually. These updating exercises take only thirty percent of the time the initial plan development required, and allow measurement of staff capacity for crystal ball gazing and implementation of mid-course corrections designed to facilitate progress in the plan's remaining years.

Planning can be one of the most wasteful, useless and unsatisfying tasks undertaken by a business organization. It can also be one of the most satisfying, rewarding and exciting functions. Unfortunately, it is more commonly the former and rarely the latter.

We believe that utilization of the orbital management theory of total participatory planning can make the satisfying, rewarding and exciting scenario a reality. Most certainly it is a goal worth working toward.

Decision Making in a Glass House

All managers develop a style for decision making which can at times be quite idiosyncratic rather than pragmatic. Whatever the method, in an orbital system it is essentially out in the open for all to see.

A hierarchical management system offers a manager the protection of rank when handing down judgmental decisions. Much as in a military organization, subordinates in a hierarchical business do not openly challenge the decision of their supervisor (though spouses, children and confidants hear of their dissatisfaction). Hierarchical managers frustrate their staffs much as a parent does who responds to a child's question of "Why?" with a simple "Because I said so."

This protection of office is stripped away in the orbital management system, where each manager is required to develop decision making procedures in clear view of individuals in the surrounding orbit. It is essentially a team effort in which the manager jeopardizes the loyalty of his staff if he uses trump cards available to his location in the system. The use of such trump cards should be held for periods of martial law, to be discussed later in this book.

Decision making in an orbit, therefore, must be exceedingly rational and thus understandable to all those who may be affected by the decision. There must be documented decision making procedures which can be followed logically by the staff. This does not entail the use of a decision matrix yielding a numerical answer, but it does require answering the question "Why?" Such an open approach to decision making may involve things as significant as employee advancement or budget allocations, more mundane subjects such as travel procedures, whether or not to send mail first or third class or how many widgets to maintain in inventory.

We have no intention of comparing employees to children in a demeaning manner, but important lessons can be learned from child development teaching. Simply stated, we have learned that children should be treated like small people with human rights and native intelligence and an ability to make significant judgments about what is right and what is wrong. Few of us treat our children that way, however, believing that because they are small and seemingly helpless they should accept our judgments without personal input. This militaristic management of children breaks down disastrously in the later years of rebellion. So too, such a management approach serves to destroy employees, not in open rebellion but in either a loss of efficiency or a failure to ever achieve the high efficiency that can only accrue to a system operated by satisfied workers.

As our world becomes more complex, mathematical models are increasingly popular for the solution of problems. But unless models are adequately documented to show how they were developed, they will be challenged and ultimately discarded. So too, decision making will fail to achieve desired results when its rationale fails to pass normal tests of human logic.

Thus, as with orbital planning, decision making in the orbital system is best viewed as a participatory procedure whenever possible.[1] This does not mean decision making by committees—a technique which most commonly produces three-humped camels—it means allowing staff members a realistic input into developing the matrix of criteria from which a decision emerges.

Obviously one item in a decision matrix will always be the intuitive judgment developed by a manager through years of experience. This wi'l be given greater or lesser weight under different circumstances, but it must never be seen as the arbitrary or capricious use of authority devoid of rational support.

Development of decisions with staff input need not be treated in a heavy-handed intensive manner through numerous, serious, and inefficient meetings. Instead it is best handled as a normal area to be addressed at periodically scheduled meetings where a wide variety of subjects are addressed. An informal if not casual approach to obtain staff input is always the best approach; it avoids too heavy a burden on employees without opinion or input on any issue.

Too detailed focus on the many facets of a management system makes that system appear structured and inflexible when just the reverse is true. Perhaps in this area of decision making, it is best that the reader recognize and absorb the form and not the substance. Once again, a cooperative management attitude is the ultimate objective of most of the significant aspects of the orbital management system. It thrives on self-starters who rankle at authoritarian systems but who experience unrestricted growth by virtue of exercisable self-determination.

Realistic examples of participatory decision making might include the addition of a staff position; the collective decision of a management unit (department, division, or group) will be far more meaningful than a unilateral decision. Similarly, work scheduling functions best with broad input. Travel procedures might also benefit from careful discussion with all affected staff.

Managers, however, will at times have to make difficult decisions on their own in full view of their working units. Not all decisions can be popular, and while the orbital management system should effectively maximize staff approval of managerial decisions, as with all organizations the unit manager's office will still be the place where the buck stops.

NOTES

[1]Decision making, exactly as with planning, should involve those who may be most affected or those who are closer to the problem; these people will clearly have a better handle on the situation.

Chapter 4 /

Efficiency Vs. Creativity

ALL SYSTEMS STRIVE TOWARD EFFICIENCY though many fail. Some systems promote creativity and most fail. There are considerable conflicts between those two objectives if they are desired simultaneously. The orbital system allows an interesting assessment of this managerial problem.

It stands to reason that employees with training and experience will be more capable and efficient in fulfilling their tasks than newer employees under supervision. It follows reasonably then that new staff members should be instructed by the senior members of the staff in the most efficient way to do their work; a procedure that will surely result in the most efficient and productive work, at least for the near term. Unfortunately, if employees are not encouraged to bring individuality to the job, the company will not benefit from the synergistic blending of different personalities and skills. The result can be an incestuous inbreeding that stifles progress. We see this in authoritarian organizations like some family-owned businesses, where the father hands down the tricks of the trade to his son and the son hands them down to his son. The result can be that the work gets done, but by methods years out of date.

Each person in a line of succession must be allowed to bring up-to-date ideas to the job, or perhaps a refreshing new approach to an old task. This may add something or it may add nothing, but by not allowing or in fact discouraging new and innovative ideas, progress is sure to be threatened.

The downside risk is of course a loss of efficiency for those allowed to foul up the job by instituting their own bad ideas, but growth can only occur if such a risk is taken. Creativity must be nurtured in a special climate which rewards productive innovation but does not punish failure nor discourage further attempts at innovation. From the short-term point of view, creativity would seem to be at odds with efficiency. We have all grown old hearing the words "Do it my way." "Why?" we ask, and receive that familiar reply, "Because that is the way it's always been done."

There is an old story about the fellow who had twenty years' experience in a certain business; on closer inspection, however, we learn he had one year of experience repeated twenty times. This will happen in any company that does not allow its staff to exercise their own individuality in the completion of their work.

Let's look for a moment at the nature of the work we are referring to. Do we speak primarily of grandiose planning at the inner orbital level of department heads—marketing plans or sales promotions? Do we speak mostly of manufacturing techniques or perhaps inventory control? Could we possibly be referring to secretaries, typists or keypunch operators? The answer is, strongly, "Yes." No job is too small, (and obviously no job is too great) to allow people considerable latitude in defining the method by which they will reach the objective established by the company.

All work is best performed with an objective orientation. Perhaps in business one can say that the end justifies the means; that is, assuming the means don't harm anyone, cost too much money or frustrate a team effort. Employees at all levels need to be made fully aware of the objective of *their* work as it relates to the company's goals. They should be advised of any time or financial requirements which must not be exceeded in the achievement of the objectives, and then be allowed to establish their own procedure. Clearly this will frustrate efficiency in many areas. Workers will follow some blind alleys and make some obvious errors. Eventually, however, efficiency will improve and progress will benefit from each individual's creative input.

Throughout this development process for each employee, his hub individual or rotational center (department head, division manager or group leader) should supply assistance and advice to the fullest extent of their ability, specifically addressed to the needs of the newer staff member. While this is not exactly the same way a law professor leads his student to the proper conclusions (through a sometimes circuitous path of logical analysis), it should have a certain air of that educational process as it leads to unusual personal growth.

Such creative indoctrination is in fact a continuing process, and can frequently produce slower initial productivity. It requires a longer period of orientation where less should be expected of new staff members, or even older members with newer jobs. But in the orbital system, with virtually no exceptions, such indoctrination leads to far more satisfied creative and productive employees. The long-run net result becomes increased efficiency. This method is analogous to investing in a more expensive car, which returns the investment because of greater durability than a less expensive car, or to investment in a new energy system which costs more initially but pays back in reduced energy costs.

The hierarchical system is cheaper and easier to implement but rarely advances beyond its initial efficiency or productivity; hierarchy commonly stunts the growth of its employees at an early stage of development.

While we have described primarily the handling of employees at the beginning of their employment, it should be emphasized that the process repeats itself as staff members expand their jobs and take on newer or increased responsibility. In either case, freedom of choice and creative initiative are always the byproduct in the orbital management system.

Chapter 5 /

Meetings: When, Where, Why?

THE MAJORITY OF MANAGERS CLASSIFY MEETINGS as their primary time-waster, yet they continue to schedule them regardless of their value or lack of value. Board meetings, as Robert Townsend once said, "are best run standing up" in a board room or, better still, treading water in a swimming pool.[1] Here lies the heart of the meeting problem, namely the people in attendance, who must wander over irrelevant subject matter, are indecisive, and disinclined toward action. There may in fact be excellent reasons for meetings but, without proper preparatory briefing of those who attend, there is no hope of success.

A hierarchical system thrives on meetings because it is a natural outgrowth of a superior exercising dominance over his subordinates. Obviously meetings are an attempt to gather and disseminate information efficiently, but they rarely achieve anything close to efficiency for a combination of the following reasons:

1) They have no orderly agenda prepared and distributed in advance.
2) They are not chaired in an effective manner.

3) Participants are allowed to ramble on about irrelevant issues.
4) Frequently too many people of only tenuous connection to the issue at hand are required to attend.[2]

Hierarchical systems employ many supervisors who do not have direct responsibility for a specific job related task; thus they have a tendency to call meetings as an important part of their job. Supervisors lose no time in a meeting but the supervised do.

In the orbital system a reverse momentum works against the calling of meetings. Everyone is busy with their own personal work. The last thing they need is the wasteful interruption of that work by an unnecessary meeting and, thus, meetings tend not to be called.

But meetings do have some value. They can be helpful in collectively threshing out a problem, or in bringing staff awareness of a subject up to par with the needs of an organizational unit.

If you hold a meeting, begin it on time no matter who is missing. Latecomers will get what they missed from those who came on time and, better still, will get the message about being prompt next time. Wait for no one; if the meeting caller is late, other attendees should turn around and go back to work. Starting precisely is not a joke or a game but a discipline. It sets the tone for the length and breadth of all meetings whose efficiency and productivity will, by the way, increase markedly.

Don't worry about where to hold short meetings. They can be held just about anywhere—offices, corridors, lunchrooms, standing or sitting. Longer agendae obviously require the more formal and spacious setting of a conference room or its equivalent.

At least once a year all departments should hold a retreat-like, open-ended meeting for a day, evening or even weekend to unload every thought and idea that may be clinging to each individual's gray matter. These meetings should provide a free-wheeling true catharsis. They must have a flexible agenda and an informal atmosphere. This type of meeting is an investment in the future. Retreats occasionally prove to be as unproductive and wasteful as most meetings but, more likely, the bottom line will be heavily in the black.

Finally, a word to meeting callers, chairpersons or whomever. Be firm and decisive! This is the one place in the orbital system where less than a dictatorial stance is wasteful. Keep the discussion on target and the people in order. Do not be shy, or surely you will lose the respect of your co-workers for wasting their time. If you can't stand the heat, don't call the meeting. Send a written communique.

Managers in the orbital system must develop a sensitivity for knowing when meetings are needed, lest they ignore such occasions to the detriment of collective activity. Meetings should be called spontaneously when a problem arises needing group attention, or when new knowledge becomes available which could be immediately acted upon by the group. Meetings should also be held periodically on a flexibly scheduled basis, perhaps once or twice a month.

An agenda should be prepared and distributed in advance to all participants, for all meetings. Don't pad the agenda to justify the meeting. A brief fifteen-minute meeting on one or two relevant subjects is far better than a one-hour meeting on ten subjects of questionable relevance.

The person who called the meeting will often be embarrassed by the speed with which its primary purpose can be carried out; commonly he will try to extend the meeting to justify calling it in the first place. Resist such idiocy. It takes very little time to assemble busy people who have no time to waste dawdling in transit, and they will be thrilled, refreshed and surprised when the meeting turns out to be short.

Call your meetings on precise minutes like 1:42—people quickly get the message that you mean business. Meetings billed as starting on the hour or half hour rarely really do; the five or ten minutes after those symmetrical points on the clock are not generally considered late.[3]

NOTES

1. Townsend, Robert. *Further Up the Organization.* New York: Alfred A. Knopf, Inc., 1984.

2. Remember participative planning and decision making.

3. Ara Parsegian used to start football practice at Notre Dame at 2:56 each afternoon and that did not mean 2:57.

Chapter 6 /

Staffing Up and Breaking In

Staffing Up

WHEN DO YOU NEED ADDITIONAL PEOPLE? How do you find and select them? Answering these questions can be difficult in the orbital system.

One of the most disconcerting problems for managers involves the addition of new staff members whose tasks are not fully defined. This occurs when we decide on a new general area of work or a "step-up" in an ongoing task. The manager believes there is enough work to justify additional staff but, upon hiring someone, finds that the details of the work to be done are not clear. In fact, the staff member may not have much to do!

A manager sincerely concerned with the efficient running of a business finds it better to have too much work than too many people. With too much work, one can be confident that no one sits idle (and no salary money is wasted). Of course, some important work may remain undone. On the other hand, there is a tendency for individuals to be less efficient under less pressure to complete their tasks; thus undercapacity produces inefficiency. A "Murphy" business management law could read "Work that doesn't need to be done right away frequently doesn't get done any way."

While this theory of "under-staffing" may seem hard on employ-ees, the vast majority of employees would far rather be busy through their work day than have periods of idle time.

With these points in mind, it is generally the best policy to add additional staff only under great pressure from other staff mem-bers who recognize that their work load is more than they can handle efficiently. Another legitimate reason would be the need to expand a particular function of one department. The work-load of a department makes it obvious when it is necessary to add staff. There should be no need for a department head to make an arbitrary decision to expand.

The reader should not interpret this concept as a desire to stay small; we do not feel that is necessarily a positive attribute. People are our greatest resource. The more people we can effectively put to work, the more productive we will be. But the key word is "effective." Too many people without enough to do cause what we call the "spaghetti syndrome." If one places a wooden pointer on a table and pushes on the handle of the pointer, the front of the pointer quickly moves forward. If you place a cooked spaghetti noodle on a plate and push on one end of the spaghetti, the other end doesn't move at all. Slackness in a business organization can result in the very same lack of response. You may have heard the saying "If you want to get something done quickly, take it to a busy person." We have found it to be true. Therefore, we always try to have an office full of busy people.

When the work load makes it obvious that additional staff members are required, the manager can easily outline ninety percent of the new staff member's job description. It will be composed of a series of tasks that can be taken from a number of overworked individuals, who should have the opportunity to unload those tasks they find least satisfying. These tasks, when added to certain new and creative functions, will adequately make up the duties of the new staff person.

Every department head or division manager should keep a list of tasks they would undertake if they had enough staff. When staff additions are finally required, these tasks can then be added to the job description. The reader should recognize this as almost organic growth—that is to say, it tends to grow of its own accord. Decisions are almost forced on managers when it comes to growth. One can argue that a manager should be able to antici-pate such growth, but we believe any organization not strangled by red tape can respond quickly to the need for staffing up; full-time employees should never be sitting around waiting for a period of overload.

The ability of employees to give less desirable tasks to new staff members is an advantage of this system of growth. This should not be considered "dumping" on a new employee, but rather the evolution of a job description for all employees which is suited to their skills and creativity. New employees do not see their tasks as someone's leftovers, but rather as a part of a new challenge. The fact that another staff member previously did some of those tasks makes that part of the job easier—they have someone to whom they can go for assistance. At the same time, let us stress that it is always advantageous to include new tasks from the manager's "wish list" in the work description of a new employee. This gives the employee a sense of innovative opportunity within the company; he will have the satisfaction of plowing new ground in some areas of his work. A recommended mix would be sixty to seventy percent of old work tasks and thirty to forty percent of new work tasks.

It is difficult to give new employees a job which is entirely new to the company. In that case, there is no one to whom they can go to gain firsthand assistance. The burden on the manager becomes extremely heavy and runs counter to the theory of the orbital system, in which every member of the staff should spend eighty percent of his time in direct individual productivity and only twenty percent of available time supervising those in an outer orbit of responsibility.

The final decision to add staff should be made by the department head with the input of those members of the staff who will be most affected by the staff addition. If present employees feel strongly that no additional staff members are needed and that they can handle the work load, their advice should be accepted. If they agree that their unit would greatly benefit by an addition, the decision for hiring should be made.

At this point, a plan for hiring an additional staff member should be adopted. This should include first advertising the opening internally, thus giving individuals opportunity to move within the orbital structure. Second, decide whether to advertise the job in the newspapers, with employment agencies, or both. Pay attention to staff recommendations of friends or associates—they are equally important. Leads obtained through staff will frequently be most effective and of the highest quality in the orbital system; when a member of the company is willing to recommend a friend, he or she has made a strong statement about both the friend and the company.

While there is always a desire to obtain the best possible person for the job, clearly a point of diminishing return is reached if too much time is spent in the interviewing process. No matter how extensive the search, hiring new employees always presents an element of risk. Once two or three acceptable candidates are located, the search committee should measure and compare candidate capabilities and make a decision. Extensive "search" procedures should be avoided whenever possible, although anyone clearly inadequate for the task at hand should never be hired.

In the orbital management system, adding a new staff member can be compared to the adoption of a child or the beginning of a marriage. It is a very important decision, not at all cold and impersonal. But, unlike adoption, it should be done expeditiously but not permanently. All new employees should be told that their hiring is probational until the company and the employee are confident that the union will be successful. Don't hesitate to admit the risk involved and the possibility that the wrong choice may have been made on one side or the other. This should be discussed candidly and a two- or three-month probationary period should be established. It is at this point that the more difficult job begins—the assimilation of a new staff member into the company.

Breaking in New Staff

The optimum technique for acclimating the new employee lies somewhere between the Welcome Wagon and a fraternity initiation. New staff should be made comfortable, but they should not get the idea that the company operates only for that purpose. Initially the department head or division manager should describe in detail the functions of the new job and the operation of the company. The procedural manual should be reviewed. Each co-worker within the group should have an opportunity to talk at length with the new staff member, describing the nature of their own job and how it interfaces with the new one. Then the new employee should be literally thrown into the job and given a fairly free hand. He should be put to work as quickly as possible in a productive capacity as there is no substitute for learning on the job. A small chance exists that people will make mistakes without proper indoctrination but it is worth the risk. The new employee should understand that he can feel free to call upon co-workers for assistance, and be encouraged to ask "dumb" questions to avoid moving straight ahead in the wrong direction.

Hierarchical systems tend to make two major errors with new employees: 1) They are apt to over-indoctrinate to the point of boredom before the individual is allowed to lay hands on actual work and 2) they tend to provide overly tight supervision in the early stages, making the person uncomfortable and insecure about his own capabilities. All staff must make it on their own eventually. In the orbital system, the beginning is a good place to start. The relaxed atmosphere of the orbital office allows for low pressure experimentation in the learning process. Self-starting, motivated, independent employees are the result.

While this "trial-by-fire" indoctrination is going on, new employees should be encouraged to spend time viewing the overall operation of the company. They should feel free to ask others about their roles in the company and to question the relationships of the different departments on a firsthand basis. Such explanations will have been made by the new employee's closest supervisor, but that form of learning is not nearly as effective as the opportunity to acquire a firsthand view.

Work tasks to be given to the new employee initially should not be of critical value. Therefore, when mistakes are made, they will not jeopardize the productivity of the organization. As the employee gains confidence in his ability to fit into the system and perform useful work, work should be increased in importance. Concurrently, the new employee should be encouraged to begin developing procedures for those areas of the job essentially new to the operation of the department. Willingness of the department head or the division manager to give a new employee opportunity to exercise creativity from the start is an excellent confidence builder. Building employee confidence is perhaps *the* most important management function, and is vitally important to the orbital system. The system, after all, depends more on individual creativity than on control of manpower by a hierarchical leader.

Brief conferences should be held between the unit manager and the new employee about once a week for the first four or five weeks. This immediate feedback will allow midcourse corrections when necessary. These conferences should be low-key and casual, with an obvious effort made to make the person feel comfortable. The manager needs to make it clear that he has two important goals: he wants the individual to truly enjoy his new place with the company, and he needs to ensure that the employee is capable of making a satisfactory contribution.

In these conferences any obvious employee weaknesses should be pointed out. Necessary training should be developed if needed, to enable all tasks to be met effectively. Training could be in the form of temporary close supervision by one or more co-workers or attendance at some formal workshop. Spending funds on formal training should generally be withheld until the end of the probationary period. At that point, the manager can be more certain that an employee will be staying with the company and that training funds will not be wasted.

If the employee's performance shines beyond all hopes during the probationary period, the manager should strongly consider an immediate favorable salary correction. Orbital management systems should not make money from their employees by getting more out of them than they pay them for. They should make money from the direct productivity of the employee. Any salary adjustments should be within the standard pay schedule of the system and will vary based on the nature of the work, the location of the company, its economic stability and the current market for the employee's particular skills.

Performance of new employees must be measured very carefully during the probationary period. If all the skeletons are brought out of the closet early, few surprises will exist once a final decision has been made to make the "adoption" relatively permanent. Don't be afraid to listen to your gut reactions; they will come back to haunt you later if you ignore them. If at the end of the probationary period the manager is unsure that the relationship between the company and the employee is going to work out, the probationary period might be extended for a month.

The one major drawback to the orbital management system (compared to the hierarchical system) is its requirement for very good people. Without motivated, self-starting individuals throughout the organization, the system will fail. For this reason, the decision to make an employee a full-fledged member of the staff is an unusually important one. Without a supervisor standing over them, unsuitable employees can cause considerably more damage than they could in a hierarchical system, where supervision is a way of life.

Chapter 7 /

Creating Your Own Job While Traveling In Orbit

Creating Your Own Job

SOCIOLOGISTS TELL US THAT FEWER THAN TWENTY-FOUR PERCENT OF THE WORK FORCE are truly satisfied with their jobs. This is an unfortunate statistic because enjoyment of one's work affords life's greatest pleasures.

Hierarchical systems place people in relatively inflexible positions where very few changes can be independently initiated. The orbital system attempts to reverse this shortsightedness.

First, a job is designed for the new employee, as described in Chapter 6. Then the employee is encouraged to maximize that portion of the job which he or she likes best, with the understanding that it will frequently be possible to eventually discard those tasks least attractive to the individual's interests and capabilities. This assumes that the employee can become so valuable performing those tasks he finds most satisfying that it actually becomes inefficient to allow him to continue performing other tasks with considerably less efficiency and skill.

Concurrently, all employees are encouraged to reach out beyond their jobs and ask for the opportunity to participate in other activities going on within the organization. Such outreach must initially be done in addition to, rather than in place of, the current work load. But once the employee proves his or her value in the new task, an opportunity will arise to trade off less desirable existing functions.

This type of job shopping requires some entrepreneurial spirit, because no creative assistance is offered to the employee from the outside. He must seek out additional creative outlets with the idea of making the total job more satisfying. The company allows and encourages this kind of activity, but does not guide it.

The system works because initially the company gets something for nothing. The employee asks to do some additional work with no immediate reward. There is a natural inclination for a manager to allow this extracurricular effort because it normally results in an overall increase in productivity. When task reassignment is required later because the employee is making a greater contribution at the newer tasks, there is still no negative impact. The net efficiency of the organization is improved because the employee has gained a higher level of job satisfaction working at tasks more suitable to his personality and skills.

In order to allow this job shaping to occur, managers must be careful not to unreasonably overload staff members; their capacity to consider additional creative outlets must not be severely curtailed.

Examples of creative job outlets may be a bookkeeper wanting an opportunity to develop a special computer program, an editor wanting to research a story, a researcher desiring to do some creative writing, a word-processing technician who would like to perform in an editing capacity, anyone wishing to work on product promotion or development programs, a manager wishing to contribute to the art department, an artist who would like to write copy, or a draftsman who thinks he could improve an engineering design.

Do not discount the value of on-the-job training which enables individuals to break out of their restricted area of work where they have been constrained by limited background experience. People learn by seeing, hearing and reading and may have a greater potential for contribution than one would ever imagine.

"Specialists" in the company may try to exercise turf control to reject contributions from those not formally trained in specific disciplines. Writers, artists and engineers will tend to reject contributions from the untrained no matter what raw merit they may contain. You will need thoughtful application of human understanding to overcome such resistance without eroding the self-confidence of any of the involved employees—Solomon-like wisdom is frequently required. The rewards are well worth the effort, however, because human growth is a bonus to both the individual and the company. Growth is too often stifled in the hierarchy, but with tender love and care it can be nurtured in the orbital system.

When an employee leaves the company, orbital managers need to look very closely at the redistribution or disposal of jobs left behind.[1] In two years, an employee has undoubtedly acquired a collection of tasks—less a product of efficient compatability of company functions than a result of personal skill and desires on the part of the individual. When such a person leaves the company, it is unlikely that his or her set of work tasks will neatly fit into a package easily transferred to either a new employee or an existing employee desiring a complete internal job change. Attempting to shift the entire work package to another often results in a non-cohesive, inefficiently-run operation.

This is an ideal time to carefully delineate those job functions and work tasks which could be claimed by existing employees who wish to broaden their base, add to their responsibilities, learn new skills, or perhaps be relieved of responsibilities they would prefer to give up if a suitable replacement could be found.

In summary, departure of a long-term employee offers a unique opportunity for job building among the remaining employees. The tasks available for selection should be widely advertised to the staff through the company's internal staff newsletter.

Sometimes a departing employee requires no replacement. The staff member who is leaving may have five primary work tasks which could be efficiently disbursed among five remaining employees who would like to add one or more tasks to their job description. Assuming that each of the existing employees has been so efficient in his current job that he can add a new task without resulting work overload, then in fact we have succeeded in eliminating a full time employee. Additionally, we have raised the productivity of existing employees without straining the operation of the company.

More likely, however, one or more employees taking on one of the tasks will eventually need assistance in some other phase of their work. It is quite likely that through this task dissemination system, the company may need to replace one-half of the lost manpower by means of a part time employee or a new employee shared by a number of departments or divisions requiring fractional manpower contributions.

It may take some time before manpower allocations are balanced and it can be determined if a net gain in efficiency or economy has resulted. But an immediate creative lift in staff morale occurs, as employees gain a unique opportunity to shape their jobs in accordance with personal interests and skills, wherever such interests and skills can be satisfied.

Inter- and Intra-Orbital Travel

Moving within a single orbit as well as from orbit to orbit is nearly without obstacle under this system, and results in a freedom of spirit which breaks the stereotyped bonds of the working world. This relates directly to the previous subject of creating one's own job—concurrent with the ability to shape a job comes the possibility of moving from unit to unit within the orbital structure, as well as the opportunity to take on different positions within a single unit or orbit.

Let us assume that one is a staff member in the payroll group of the accounting division of the business management department. The payroll group has a group leader and two staff members, and one staff member wants to participate in the accounts receivable group working also for that group leader. Depending on work loads, this option would probably exist; the individual could discuss it with the accounting division manager and probably be able to work in two different orbits within his own larger orbital system.

The same payroll employee might also wish to work in the orbit of a completely different department, perhaps as a part-time draftsman in the drafting group of the graphics division of the publications department. The orbital system would make every effort to allow him to fulfill his creative desires through different outlets as long as the end result to the company remains a highly efficient output.

High efficiency in such a mobile system is not easily reached without considerable planning, manipulation, coordination, and sometimes outright juggling. There will always be obstacles in the form of other individuals who do not want people crossing boundaries. Proper indoctrination into the system, however, will make everyone recognize that they themselves benefit by encouraging the potential for inter- and intra-orbital travel which allows a high level of job satisfaction throughout all working careers in the orbital management system.

Even more important in orbital travel is the opportunity given an individual to jump into the center of his own orbit, going from staff member of one group to group leader in a totally different orbit, or into an orbit of rotation around the very same division manager. For instance, the very same member of the payroll group may want an opportunity to develop a computerized payroll deduction system which allows employees to have certain fixed bills paid automatically out of their paychecks, as banks may do for electric bills or mortgage bills. The payroll staff member might present this idea to the accounting division manager and ask for an opportunity to work out a procedure. If planning and development of the payroll deduction product look fruitful, the division manager might give the payroll staff member the opportunity to form a payroll deduction group and be its leader, initially without other staff, but ultimately (if the program is beneficial and requires additional assistance) becoming leader of a staffed group. Thus, inter-orbital movement would be spawned from one's own creativity.

Such lateral and vertical movement is rarely possible in a more rigid hierarchical system. Within a hierarchy, movement generally occurs only where vacancies develop both laterally and vertically. Individuals can then apply to fill those vacancies with either different jobs at the same level or different jobs at higher levels. This is a more orderly system of movement, but it does not allow for creative development or increased job satisfaction—one can get stuck in a rut very quickly and often does. Someone once said that a rut was a grave with the ends kicked out. Well there are no ruts in the orbital system.

Inter- and intra-orbital travel are very important aspects for insuring creative growth. Readers may argue that all workers are not creative, and that a company can't be filled with people who want to move sideways and up while accepting different challenges. They might say that many people are more suited to fit into one job and to continue that way without dissatisfaction. Many workers do end up in one fairly structured slot, but we have yet to find one person who truly enjoyed it. People rationalize their plight in such a job—say that everything is fine and that they are satisfied—simply because they have no options. But given a truly viable option to focus on, few people can be found who do not have more to offer than they are in fact contributing in a given time on the present job.

We have been talking about orbital travel in a structural sense but there is something to be said for it in a literal sense: that is to say, the ability and capacity for individuals to physically move within an organization, to have an opportunity to visit with other people to find out what's being done in other jobs, and to see if they could contribute something given the opportunity. Such an opportunity—on company time—can obviously lead to wasted time, useless visiting, or elongated coffee breaks. Few things in life cannot be taken advantage of, but with the right atmosphere and the right environment one can minimize the cheaters or abusers (who are dealt with in a later chapter) and maximize the positive benefits of flexibility.

Of course there are times when inter-orbital travel of the physical nature is not desirable. In any business there are periods of crisis and turmoil created by a major alteration in structure or procedures of critical business tasks. This may be as mundane as changes in word processing procedures, mail room procedures, or graphic development, or as critical as the alteration of an accounting system. Periods such as these (described in the chapter on "Martial Law") are times when staff cannot be granted the same opportunities for either physical or job expansion orbital travel. No system or concept works all the time; thus each must be suspended at some time. That does not mean they are not sound and valuable procedures. Detractors of the flexible orbital system will take pleasure in pointing to these periods of difficulty as an indication of system failure but their arguments are not valid. Size is, of course, a factor in the ability of people to move readily within the organizational structure to satisfy their creative desires and apply their productive skills. But while we do not suggest the orbital structure for all businesses, the chapter on optimum size will show that the system is quite capable of working within an organization larger than 300 people.

NOTES

1. Leaving is normally a result of relocation of a spouse, return to school, retirement, or unmatchable salary competition elsewhere. Attrition due to discontent is unusual for an employee who has been in the system for more than two years.

Chapter 8 /

Clerks and Typists No More

INDIVIDUALS CEASE TO FEEL LIKE WARM-BLOODED MACHINES when they are offered an exceptionally high level of self-determination in the fulfillment of various functions and tasks. Titles that accompany such attitudes then become obsolete.

Clerks and typists are a particularly good example of this problem. To call someone a clerk or a typist certainly does not describe in any substantial manner what that individual does for the benefit and productivity of an organization. It tells us, of course, that one person does clerical work and is called a clerk and that another strikes the keys of a typewriter and is called a typist, but these are very nondescript titles and do not help us in describing the substantial contribution of an individual. Most clerks or typists handle a wide variety of clerical and typing tasks, and no single description of their work fully describes all the projects in which they participate. But more than likely, one or more main tasks which the individual takes pride in carry the highest priority for the organization, and would better describe what that person does.

In the orbital system we attempt to offer each individual an absolute minimum of autonomy equal to thirty percent of their effort. That means that individuals are promised the opportunity

to make significant decisions affecting at least thirty percent of
their work. These decisions may vary from deciding how typed
material is formatted, how recorded material is filed, or how a
variety of jobs are prioritized, to the total determination of how
an end product will be achieved. When managers find that
employees gain the most satisfaction from those tasks over which
they have the greatest decision making capabilities, they may
consider giving a title to an employee which describes his particular tasks. For instance, in a word processing division it may be best
to assign word processing technicians to various areas of specialization. If an organization has departments with different needs—
a business department, a research department, or a publications
department—the word processing needs are significantly different. Members of the word processing division may be assigned to
spend part of their time specializing in insuring the accurate
production of work for one particular department. They might
not do only that department's work, but where possible they
would be assigned to it. So for illustrative purposes, an employee
in the word processing division, instead of being called a typist or
a word processing machine operator, might be titled a "research
manuscript coodinator," or a "publications preparation director."
This may sound a bit stilted to some readers but it is important in
terms of the self-image one develops through a job. It is even
possible to assert that an employee is not being properly managed
if one cannot come up with a special title that properly describes a
significant portion of his or her work. If an employee functions in
a nondescript manner, always doing bits and pieces of things
where the whole is never understood, he will never develop full
potential, no matter what that potential may be. The same would
be true of a posting clerk in an accounting department. Some
things being posted will be more important than others. There is
always some area where the employee may be offered an opportunity to see more than a small functional part of a task; where he
can be given an opportunity to specialize, to be creative, to make
an individual contribution and thus gain a title. In publications,
an employee may work as a paste-up artist—for publication after
publication. Most people would not want to go through life as a
paste-up artist. We are convinced that every individual like this
spends a relatively important part of his time pasting up some
particular type of document on a regular basis; he could instead
make a larger contribution to the production of that document
and gain a title.

   The orbital management system is founded on the basis of a
sincere desire to allow each and every employee to make a special,

personal contribution to an organization. Admittedly, the system frequently contradicts the preaching of hierarchical systems organized in a strongly functional structure. A functional organization groups everyone doing similar tasks together and does not allow for individuals carrying projects through from beginning to end. That organizational approach is called categorical. Functional organization lends itself to mechancial tasks requiring minimal creativity, while categorical organizations work best where creative contribution can continually improve upon the end product. While one can argue that the most efficient factory should be set up functionally, there is little to support such an argument for a non-manufacturing business organization. Modern management is even learning that productivity increases in factories when workers can watch a machine develop from a frame to a complete entity. The Volvo Corporation of Sweden pioneered this methodology.

Most organizations find a mixture of functional and categorical delineations to be ultimately most efficient. We cannot argue the validity of a word processing department where many people sit side by side and operate word processing machines. We cannot argue the validity of a graphics department where artists work side by side developing art material for various publications. We are insisting that each of these people can to some extent be given a specialization which will allow them to be more fully involved in the productivity of a task from its beginning to end, to deal with the people who conceived the idea, and to carry it along toward the graphics contribution, the word processing department, and beyond. Every worker can be given a chance to see himself as a part of a special team at some point.

Managers who work with their employees can mutually develop this kind of job integration. It may seem cumbersome to a manager initially because it takes more thoughtful planning, but we promise that it will result in greater productivity, increased employee satisfaction, and will forever eliminate clerks and typists.

Avoiding Negative Descriptors

Functional hierarchical classifications also frequently carry negative connotations and create self-fulfilling mind sets which stifle productivity and growth. While this concern may seem to be more with form than substance, words that fall into this category must be expunged from common use.

A title, which a person brings to the job each day and carries home in a similar manner, has a great deal to do with determining his state of mind and the importance he places on himself and his position in a company. Let us focus on the elimination of relatively meaningless low-level employee titles, and suggest substituting some reasonable description of what an employee really does during a significant amount of his time. It is our desire here to broaden the discussion to a variety of other titles and non-titles as well as classifications of general working groups.

We used to laugh when janitors of buildings became maintenance engineers, when bowling alleys became bowling lanes, or when garbage men became sanitation workers. But these things are not funny to the individuals or proprietors whom they affect. Negative descriptors have a great deal to do with how we feel about ourselves and our businesses, and how others feel about us.

Today typing pools, secretarial pools, and stenographic pools are being replaced by word processing departments or staff services. Indeed, these titles signify more than just an intent to make something simple sound more complex. In today's electronic world we are very definitely talking about word processing or automatic typing equipment, advancing to the point where dedicated computers are the rule rather than the exception in most reasonably sized companies. Individuals who manage word processing divisions need to be and are highly skilled; they wish that their departments would receive the recognition they deserve.

At the other end of the spectrum, we are always amused by some of the more grandiose titles given to top level administrators in the Federal Government—for example, Associate Deputy Assistant Administrator for Solid Waste in the Environmental Protection Agency. In the federal hierarchical structure terms are constantly strung together—Associate Deputy Assistant, Assistants to Assistants, Deputies to Deputies, Acting, and so on—into the night. These titles tell one little, but to some extent they belittle extremely high-level responsible positions held by individuals and ensure that superiors, inferiors and peers within the government know exactly at which level of the hierarchy each individual resides.

In the Orbital System it is much more important for a title to describe exactly what a person does than where that person sits within the structure of responsibility and power.

The term Assistant-to (anyone or anything) as title is a very good example of a negative descriptor. The immediate perception is that spending one's life assisting another within a corporate structure is less rewarding and less satisfying (if not, in fact, demeaning) than holding some specific responsibility of one's own. All of us, at one time or in one part of our job, assist someone or some group to a significant extent. But if an organization is getting the most from an individual, that individual must also hold full responsibility for some area of activity, perhaps an area where overall responsibility belongs to the person the individual is "Assistant-to." Why demean with a title indicating subservience, when it is possible to indicate that part of the job for which an individual is truly responsible, whether or not he answers to a higher-up. Which one of us does not answer to higher-ups in all of our work, in some form or another?

Get rid of "Assistant-to's," get rid of "Deputies." Let people be known for what they really do. Recognize that a negative descriptor to one individual may not be a negative descriptor to another. Some people may be proud to carry the title "secretary." Others are offended by the term and feel they are more important and are, in fact, administrative assistants. Sometimes the term "secretary" is more appropriate; at other times administrative assistant may be more accurate. It depends upon the level of responsibility carried by that individual in their supportive work for another executive. We believe, within reason and where possible, that each individual should have the right to determine his or her title—secretary, administrative assistant, or a more specific title describing some facet of the work which is their sole responsibility.[1] Most workers have multiple responsibilities and could carry many titles. In the Orbital System, this is always true for the chief operating officer, for all department heads, and often for division managers. Because it is cumbersome to carry more than one title, everyone generally should be given a single title or the opportunity to choose one. Titles should become shorter as one approaches the orbit's center—head of the business department, head of the research department, or chief operating officer. As we move further out into orbit, the title might be longer to describe a specific task—for example, "manuscript formatting coordinator."

Sometimes a title will not tell us immediately exactly what a person does. But that isn't always detrimental. Is it so terrible to give your occupation or job title and to be asked, "Well, what does that mean?" The question provides an opportunity to explain in detail what you really do. We think it leads to a more interesting conversation than when you say, "I'm just a secretary" and leave it at that.[2]

Examples are endless. A warehouseman may be more involved in inventory control than anything else; he might choose to be known for that aspect of his work. A key puncher feeding data into a computer may be primarily involved in some very significant research projects or accounting programs; he might prefer to be known for that aspect of his work. The point is, individuals in the Orbital System are given an opportunity to be known specifically for what they do. This allows them to develop greater pride and satisfaction in recognizing the important role that they play in a system where, for the most part, everyone is equal except on payday.

Negative descriptors come in all shapes and sizes and may not be recognized by everyone. But a sensitive organization will make an effort to ensure that negative descriptors are eliminated on the most personal level.

CO_2—Sans Secretary or Do You Really Need a Secretary Anyway?

If you had difficulty decoding this subtitle, we will quickly clear up the confusion. CO_2 is another symbol we use for Chief Operating Officer, and "sans" is a French word meaning "without" commonly used as an English idiom. CO_2 is a particularly fitting symbol because, as most people recognize, it is also the chemical symbol for carbon dioxide—a primary component of the hot air commonly expelled from all of us and particularly from those in officious kinds of positions.

Officiousness is a flaw found in all levels of a hierarchy. One can make a case for it being worse at lower levels, but here we shall deal with it only at the top, and then briefly. In fact, we should dismiss it instantly because, if it is a pervasive quality of the CO_2, the entire orbital management system can come tumbling down or, more appropriately, fly apart.

The air of equality, of democracy[3] in action at the real life orbital management level, must be evident from the center of the system on out to the most distant orbits. The CO_2 must be visible, unpompous, and self-effacing. In addition, he must exhibit the qualities of a dedicated, untiring worker.

All these desirable traits and attributes can frequently be masked by the CO_2's secretary, whose officiousnous can be enough for her and for her boss as she fills the well-known office position of Queen Bee.[4] Of course, not all secretaries to CO_2's fit that description or in any way detract from the orbital system; enough do, however, to make elimination of the job worth considering.

Readers may consider this recommendation as perhaps revolutionary and even unrealistic, but it is not original. Robert Townsend in *Further Up The Organization*[5] suggested that Chief Operating Officers use the typing pool instead of a secretary and make their own telephone calls and airline reservations, but Townsend's idea never caught on. We recommend a variation on that theme that has even more practical benefits than Townsend's idea.

We believe he failed to attract a following because his concept lacked personal involvement between the CO_2 and the person or persons performing secretarial duties. This can be remedied by eliminating a personal secretary to the CO_2 and substituting his use of all department secretaries. Each department head will have a single secretary or administrative assistant (a term we dislike) to aid in the smooth management of the department work. All work from a department beyond the capacity of the department head's secretary should go to the word processing division (or staff services) housed somewhere within the organization. Analysis of any CO_2's work quickly shows that at least eighty percent relates to one or another of his operating departments. Under the usual system, copies of his correspondence to the various areas eventually will find their way to the appropriate department where additional follow-up is invariably required. The "CO_2 sans secretary" idea brings correspondence to the door of the proper departmental secretary at the beginning instead of second hand. It also brings the CO_2 in closer contact with each department in the normal course of a day, week, or month, and makes the orbital system more visible and more creditable. Any portion of work not clearly related to a department should not be imposed on a department secretary, but instead should be detailed to one individual in the word processing department (or staff services) who can serve as a part-time aide for the CO_2 during a particular project or venture.

The CO_2 can alternate between going to the appropriate department secretary or calling the secretary to his or her office. The additional work (when divided up among four to seven departmental secretaries) will not add significantly to their load and will be enjoyed and appreciated by the department secretary because of its variety. Secretaries will appreciate becoming involved with the CO_2's work, and gain satisfaction from the additional contribution they make.

Interchange between the CO_2 and the department will become visible to the entire staff of the department, and any mystery about what the CO_2 is up to tends to disappear. This exercise brings the CO_2 onto the plane of the departmental organization where he should be in the orbital system, and does away with hierarchical remnants.

There is a potential for reduced efficiency on the part of the CO_2 as he spreads the work throughout a group rather than centralizing it with one individual. But the advantages of his additional opportunity to act as the system's lubricant far outweigh the apparent mechanical inefficiency of working through many people instead of one. One can indeed argue that the proper dissemination of firsthand information is increased by this method. The possibility for inefficiency by a CO_2's secretary is also eliminated—inefficiency which is often a result of a heavy travel schedule that leaves a secretary or administrative assistant too often with idle hands and the opportunity to exercise a propensity toward Queen Beeism.

Let's look at the advantages and disadvantages of this admittedly unorthodox concept.

Advantages:

1. It eliminates one relatively highly paid staff member, and allows the work load to be absorbed by a group which increases its efficiency in the absorption process.

2. It brings departmentally-oriented information into the proper department immediately.

3. It eliminates invisible barriers between departments and the CO_2.

4. It offers a built-in information retrieval and communications system between the CO_2 and departments.

5. It greatly improves recognition of the credibility and feasibility of the orbital management system. The CO_2 is involved every day in a low-key way.

6. It requires more physical exercise, as the CO_2 moves through departmental offices.

7. It takes the CO_2 off a pedestal which exists in hierarchy but must not exist in the orbital system and makes him more human and less mysterious on close inspection.

8. The CO_2 must be self-effacing.

Disadvantages:

1. It requires more of the CO_2's time to complete correspondence.
2. It requires expenditure of more physical energy, as he moves through the organization.
3. Reaction time for completion of some urgent task can be slowed on occasion.[6]
4. It is more difficult for an outside caller to find the appropriate substitute to talk with in the absence of a CO_2[7].
5. The CO_2 must be self-effacing.

Finally, let us stress the last disadvantage though we don't truly believe it to be one. The CO_2 must be self-effacing. He cannot be a pompous ass. He must have enough self-confidence in his ability, the system, and the program not to need the ceremonial trappings of office. He can retain the high esteem of his co-workers, and involve himself in all orbits of the operation, as he meets with a multitude of the staff. They will pay him much respect but no homage, and will see him as a person with a job to do and a desire to get it done as efficiently and as effectively as possible.

NOTES

1. This latter approach is better than the former.
2. But socializing is another matter.
3. Not in the idealistic or radical sense.
4. We do recognize that a male can fill the role of a secretary, however, in the majority of present situations, this is not the case.
5. Townsend, Robert. *Further Up the Organization.* New York: Alfred A. Knopf, Inc., 1984.
6. Normally the use of more than one individual (either departmental secretaries or staff services) speeds up reaction time.
7. At times this may be an advantage, although it could be easily avoided by establishing a duty roster to cover CO_2 absences and by keeping switchboard staff fully informed.

Chapter 9 /

Absenteeism, Sick Leave and the Working Day: A New Look at Old Procedures

A REASONABLY SUCCESSFUL ORBITAL SYSTEM can institute a variety of refreshing and beneficial personnel practices which will minimize necessary sick leave, all but eliminate absenteeism, and maximize employee enthusiasm. The first and foremost requirement for the reduction of sick leave and absenteeism is the institution of a flex-time system which allows each employee to work those hours of the day which are most suitable to individual temperament and personal schedules. This means that some employees may choose to come in early and leave early, others will come in late and leave late. Some may even choose to work a block of hours early in the day and a block of hours late, with a lengthy period off at mid-day.

Since nearly all employees have to spend some period of time each day with their co-workers, some standard requirements of time input must be made. This is normally done by allowing employees to choose essentially any eight working hours out of a standard twelve-hour working day (the most common twelve-hour period would be from 7:00 a.m. to 7:00 p.m.). A twelve-hour schedule insures that virtually the entire staff of a department will spend nearly four hours of their work day together, while allowing maximum flexibility for hourly selection by each individual. Flex-time is the basis of the system which offers each employee considerable latitude in controlling working life. It has proved so effective throughout the nation today that even some of the most restrictive hierarchical management programs have adopted it. Building on flex-time, let's look at some even more innovative procedures which contribute to employee autonomy as well as company efficiency.

Most hierarchical business systems offer employees ten days sick leave each year, and analysis indicates that the average number of days sick per employee in these companies is in fact the same. One might then assume that companies give ten days of sick leave annually because most people tend to be sick that much. That, however, would not be an accurate assessment. People take ten days sick leave each year because these days are offered by their companies. Whether sick or not, most people will feign illness at least that often to take advantage of this (so-called) employee benefit, and taking advantage is indeed an accurate description. Unfair advantage might be a better statement.

Totally honest employees would and should take off only those days on which they are truly too ill to work, but in the hierarchical system, such behavior is unfortunately rare. In the orbital management system, the number of sick days averaged by employees can be shown to be well under ten days when a policy of no automatic sick days is adopted. The orbital management sick leave policy states that when an employee is too sick to work, he should take the day off and will be fully compensated. If an employee is seriously ill for an extended period of time even beyond ten days, he will still be compensated. This is a very reassuring policy. It is more tolerant and advantageous than the arbitrary ten-day sick leave policy, but employees are warmly persuaded not to take advantage of the policy by staying out of work on days when they could, in fact, make a significant contribution. We all get head colds that create a decline in our efficiency. We all have days where we feel downright depressed and unable to fulfill our greatest working potential. But from a company standpoint, an employee able to operate at fifty percent of potential capacity is still making a significant contribution beyond zero—the input to the company when an employee stays at home. The orbital system procedure encourages employees to come to work, and recognizes that they may be present more in body than in spirit. In return it offers the warm sympathy of fellow workers. This has a significantly positive impact on the psychological well being of the employee and at the same time does not demand a sick individual's fullest potential contribution. Some way to let staff members know when an employee is not feeling up to par is needed to make this system work. This can be done very simply by putting a plaque or sign on the employee's desk which reads, "I am sick."[1] It may sound silly, but it really works. Employees are impressed by the dedication of a person who comes to work not feeling his best. They offer sympathy without causing the sick employee to explain repeatedly what the problem is, and they recognize that they cannot expect full potential output from the sick person on that particular day or days. We invariably hear from employees that keeping busy is superior to wandering aimlessly about one's home in a depressed state.

There are some exceptions. In the name of health (and a healthy staff), an employee who suspects that he carries a contagious illness or disease should stay at home. With common colds, the most credible medical journals have shown that once an individual exhibits symptoms, he is no longer a contagious carrier. Most doctors now believe that continued activity at a reduced level during sick periods contributes to the physical well being of the individual. This should obviously not be interpreted as a recommendation that people so sick that they cannot stand up without being dizzy come to work. We have no intention of carrying this policy to the point of absurdity. The objective is to minimize lost time for marginal illness and depression—time when a significant contribution can be made to the company while recognizing that that contribution will be well below maximum potential. In our experience, this policy, once accepted by the staff, is looked upon very positively. The number of sick leave days actually taken by the average staff member drops well below ten. Down time in the various departments over a year is also significantly reduced, while at the same time, every employee benefits from the recognition that when, in fact, they are seriously ill and must miss work, they will be supported by the company to the fullest extent. When an employee misses a full month of work because of serious illness, other staff members see that he received full compensation and sympathy from the company. This lends credibility to the program and develops an honest, forthright staff attitude toward this healthy and positive sick leave program.

Orbital management takes a similar approach when employees need to meet personal commitments outside the company. Absenteeism often occurs when employees take time from work to fulfill personal commitments—appointments with doctors, dentists, barber shops, beauty salons—or when they must attend a child's play, an athletic event, or other occasions. Companies without heart rarely look obligingly upon such commitments; employees thus become reticient about openly asking for such time off. Instead, they simply take the time off, either as sick leave or straight absenteeism. Because this is unplanned absence, its negative impact on the company is magnified. In the orbital management system, an extremely flexible attitude is taken toward such personal commitments. Employees may freely take such time off by simply telling the co-workers who will be affected by their absence. The employees are asked only to make up the time in the normal course of the next few working days. This attitude is the heart of the orbital management system. It is not often taken advantage of, and results in an all but negligible absenteeism rate. The procedure instills a confidence in employees that eliminates the need to cheat.

One of the more exciting policies which is an extension of this flexible attitude toward personal employee commitments is the institution of what we call the "Hooky Day" procedure. There are some days at work when an employee, for one reason or another, valid or not, would prefer having the afternoon off from work. It might be a spring day when it's just too beautiful outside to remain indoors, a winter day when the ski slopes call, or an afternoon when one feels like curling up with a good book. Whatever the reason, if it will not negatively impact upon the employee's department, division or group, he can fill out a hooky slip which says he is taking the afternoon off with the proviso that time missed will be made up before his next hooky afternoon.

This procedure works as an outstanding safety valve, allowing employees to truly be captains of their fortunes, the masters of their fates. We have found that the privilege is never abused and, in fact, is used only infrequently. Knowing that he has the freedom to leave work[2] without need of any special cause or excuse, an employee develops a sense of freedom and well being which greatly contributes to his enthusiasm and dedication toward the company and its goals. The key word here again is "autonomy." The more that individuals recognize autonomy and self-determination in their working lives, the more productive and satisfied they will be. That philosophy is threaded through all aspects of the orbital management system.

NOTES

1. Or "I have a cold," etc.
2. Within the realm of reason or without abusing the system.

Chapter 10 /

Advancement on Merit

The Peter Principle Eliminated

WHEN DR. LAURENCE J. PETER penned his now famous work *The Peter Principle,* in 1969, corporate America learned why so many of its organizational charts packed with dead end slots were filled with marginally productive, insecure executives with no future further up the organization. Individuals competent to fulfill a particular assignment and historically successful with it had been promoted up the hierarchial ladder, with no particular consideration for the proper match between talent and ability and the new tasks to be performed at the next rung of the ladder.

Because such an individual had performed well and confidently in his previous position, no room was allowed for even questioning the wisdom of advancement. In corporate America, it's surprisingly un-American not to continue working one's way up the organization. But often the vertical climb leads an individual from an area of complete competence to one of limited or no competence. Here the employee, mechanically assigned, accepts the promotion without challenge, reaches his level of incompetence that creates an impediment to productivity for both himself and the organization, and never admits his failings or considers the possibility of a return to the former position of competence because of the stigma such a backward step would carry. The individual may well ride out his retirement in what quickly becomes a stagnant hallway in the corporate maze.

Orbital management eliminates this habitual failure of the hierarchial system by eliminating the inflexible path of advancement—as has been stressed earlier, advancement is largely self-determined through the creation of additional responsibility. In the orbital system, an individual advances less often into another's job. Instead, he acquires enough additional responsibility to achieve full equality of responsibility with other co-workers.

It is a cliché of big business that individuals fight their way up the corporate ladder in a competitive manner symbolic of guerrilla warfare. For some this survival of the fittest approach seems to strengthen the leadership of a company, but more often it creates an atmosphere of hostility and distrust that reduces collective productivity in the face of internal competition.

The lack of clear career paths in the orbital system might be seen as ultimately reducing motivation to achieve higher goals. This is not necessarily true. Reward is always available in the form of increased pay and responsibility, with none of the limits of size or direction that a hierarchy has. Stagnation is always a possibility, but it is easily recognized by those who depend on the services of people in a rotating unit. Individuals who have apparently ceased to grow are urged by those who depend on them to stretch personal capacities for their own benefit and that of their co-workers. Otherwise company productivity will suffer. A stagnating employee ultimately feels out of place and leaves voluntarily or is eased out by the group, which recognizes that those individuals not continuing to grow with their co-workers become too much of a liability to everyone's future success. Here we mean growth not only into new areas but also growth in the effectiveness, efficiency and technique of an individual's ability. There is no predetermined limit to the growth of any employee. Orbital management fosters that individual growth, but only in the direction of unquestioned capacity and desire. This is unlike Dr. Peters' recognition that corporate avenues too often force people to achieve their level of incompetence.

In the chapter on creating one's job, we pointed out that an orbital system manager has the opportunity to take additional responsibilities, in his area of expertise or outside it. This added responsibility allows an individual to delve into an area where his competence is questionable but his creativity may be high. With the assistance of co-workers, he can learn new skills or aspects of the organization without sacrificing competence in a particular area or without "abandoning ship" in one orbit to accommodate oneself in another. An individual can progress slowly into an area where initially he had little workable knowledge. Under this system, a person can explore many areas within the organization, but the likelihood of any worker assuming a totally new job where he has no expertise is almost non-existent. The system will not allow it. As we suggest, co-workers will not allow one person to bring the organization to a grinding halt; rather an incompetent staff member will be eased out of the system if he should resist or be quickly made aware of the uncomfortable situation. So the system allows personal growth within each individual's abilities, and reduces the chances of anyone being immersed in a job situation over their head.

The Good, the Bad and the Educated

An air of equality permeates the orbital system and results in an unusual competition between the self-made employee and those who are college-educated. It is truly heartening in the orbital management system to recognize the opportunity of giving a broad range of individuals an opportunity to advance in some special area of expertise (in which they may or may not have been trained, but in which they recognize a sincere interest and enthusiasm). While many jobs require a degree of training, many can be learned on the job. Additionally, what we consider training need not be the formal variety which offers some type of certification—a college degree or a vocational education certificate. Experience may be the best teacher, but desire is the greatest motivator and under many circumstances can make up for major voids in an individual's background. The relaxed atmosphere of an orbital company, with few rules, regulations or preconceived dogmas, allows managers to offer diverse individuals an opportunity to succeed far beyond that normally available in the rigid hierarchical corporate world. Peers of any employee tend to accept whatever tools an individual brings to a job, whether expert experience or simply a quick mind and tremendous drive. This is not generally true in a hierarchical structure. There the peers of any new employee tend to inspect his resume closely, hoping to discover every possible chink in his armor. Employees in an orbital system are apt to have more self-confidence; this reduces their need to look down upon fellow workers in order to feel superior, and makes it possible to add diversity to the staff. A manager may be as likely to fill a position with a Ph.D. as with a college dropout. A person's past is held neither for nor against him. What counts is an individual's attitude here and now, his drive to succeed, his desire to achieve, his basic intelligence, his aptitude for certain types of work and, frequently as important as anything, the position he wishes to occupy on a learning curve. That is, an ideal employee is often the person who is most comfortable learning new information—a person who is challenged by new ideas rather the employee who wants to repeat the already learned and familiar.

Managers must set the tone for this kind of hiring practice. They must neither offer automatic credit to those with proven credentials nor view the learner as a second class citizen. When people start a job they all start even. Obviously the formally trained will be expected to produce more initially. Learners should be given a little more time to prove themselves. But eventually, the same is expected of everyone; no one rests on their laurels or is expected to jump through hoops and over obstacles, in an effort to constantly live down some void in background education. One true though perhaps cornball motto of an orbital employment program is always, "Good people are hard to find." When you find them you hire them; you do not worry too much about whether they fit perfectly in a complex set of current staff requirements. Most managers soon learn to recognize that good people somehow find a way to fit wherever opportunity knocks.[2]

The orbital system allows managers to hire the untrained, and lets them learn on the job and work side by side with a degreed employee without fear of conflict. Such a system does not develop by osmosis. It is instilled in each and every employee at the time of hiring and reinforced continually as staff needs change and grow.

In this diversity of education, the engineer can work side by side with a vocationally educated high school graduate. The graduate of a formal university arts program can work closely with a high school or college drop-out with intense drive and the natural ability to be a creative artist. A graduate of the school of hard knocks may manage a department of individuals with graduate degrees; a secretary can challenge her boss for his job and win. It is a no-holds-barred free-for-all for excellence, with few points given for past achievement or attainment. In orbital management only the here and now really counts—no one leaves laurels around for anyone to rest on.

So we've made a case for the presence of a wide variety of educational levels—the highly educated and the less educated. But what do we mean by the good and the bad? The reader can take it literally and symbolically. The orbital staff will likely be a true mix of what we all consider the good and highest minded people and (some might consider) the bad or free spirits whose drive for higher levels of achievement may be questionable. Symbolically, good may stand for bright and bad may represent the slow mind. There is room for all kinds in an effective, efficient organization. The highly moral and the amoral can all work side by side and be enriched by the contacts one way or the other. Not all jobs require a high degree of intelligence. Sometimes a pleasing personality and a good attitude are the most important attributes for some jobs.

We do not mean to imply that any personality or character trait can live happily ever after within the orbital management system. Nothing could be further from the truth. The list of totally unacceptable characteristics in orbital management is a fairly long one. It includes traits such as laziness and slothfulness, and covers people who are clockwatchers, petty complainers, office politicians, duty shirkers, bad-seed planters, and phonies, and a host of others that any office can do without.

A particularly humane aspect of orbital management is taken from the Japanese employment concept where companies do not so much hire individuals as adopt them. Hiring someone can be compared to the old Chinese proverb about saving an individual's life; in China, the savior is considered responsible for the life he saved. In orbital management, the manager who does the hiring is considered responsible for the employee he hires whether that individual is successful or not. Lack of employee success is seen as the result of poor judgment on the part of the manager. It follows logically that every effort should be made to ultimately find a successful position for the adopted individual.[3] Most people have redeeming qualities that can benefit a company—it is the manager's responsibility to find the proper slot for all the pegs. The orbital management system thrives on self-starters whose enthusiasm pervades the atmosphere of the office. When an individual appears incapable of carrying out the job to which he is assigned, it is incumbent upon the manager to find him a more suitable job.[4] Generally, lack of ability or incompetence should not be grounds for termination. If an individual is good enough to hire initially, there is probably a place where he can contribute within the organization. The atmosphere of an orbitally-managed company should be charged with energy and readily apparent to outsiders making even a brief visit. The chief operating officer should regularly visit all parts of the company to monitor corporate energy levels—they will be as identifiable as radiation in the presence of a Geiger counter.

Individuals in an orbital system recognize the almost endless opportunities. This recognition keeps their frustration down and their drive to achieve at a peak. The good, the bad, and the educated can indeed be a synergistic combination of individuals.

NOTES

1. Peter, Laurence J. and Raymond Hull. *The Peter Principle*. New York: Morrow, 1969.
2. Adaptation regarding people and business situations is one of the important aspects of the orbital management system.
3. As long as compatibility and efficiency are not sacrificed.
4. Within the objectives of the organization.

Chapter 11 /

Nepotism: A New Look

NEPOTISM HAS LONG BEEN CONSIDERED A TABOO. The orbital management system not only proves that it is workable but, in fact, makes a strong case for the active development of nepotism within a corporate structure. Somewhere in the Industrial Revolution the work force got away from the family affair. We started in the family firm or family business but ended up in a cold, often impersonal, business operation where relatives were neither welcomed nor allowed. Business productivity became the overriding goal and family ties within a company were seen to have downside risks which outweighed any positive benefits of offering a source of additional skilled employees.

Generally speaking, anti-nepotism rules stem from arbitrary impressions that the hiring of relatives is detrimental to the organizational health of a business or corporation. While some rules date from the 1930s Depression attitude that no family should earn two incomes in the face of rampant unemployment, most are not founded on even this much sound reason.

The orbital system will lead the way back to the family affair in the future. While clearly the status of being an employee's relative should of itself offer no advantage in one's effort to win a job, it should be no deterrent. If worthy candidates for company positions are available and eager to work, they should be given every opportunity to compete for the position even though they are relatives of an employee. When a family member wins a job in fair competition, the company truly wins, too. This is so because the evidence of family relatives working capably within a company generally enhances the capacity for warm relationships among staff.

No one questions that it is unwise to hire any unqualified person, and we recognize the suspicions that some managers will hire a relative for other than good business reasons. But how many business leaders are self-destructive enough to hire people whose contribution would be questionable at best and destructive at worst?—the truth is, few indeed. We believe that the negatives of nepotism are founded in myth and suspicion rather than fact.

In this day and age, people are quick to notice when a company does not restrict the hiring of family members in a closed office environment, though such restrictions are less common in factory assembly lines. Employees will normally see this relaxation of what is thought by many to be an arbitrary rule as a sign of flexible, forward-looking management. They will welcome the opportunity to recommend a relative or member of their immediate family in the future and frequently will, and as more family ties are built up in this way, the entire company will come to resemble a family or series of departmental families.

We tend to think of nepotism in the context of a boss hiring his son. That opportunity does not exist throughout a business organization, and can hardly be regarded as a universal threat. When it does happen, the business is generally family-owned and such a succession is considered normal.

The inherent fear in hiring an employee's relative is that the hiring won't work out, and that the subsequent firing or dehiring may create a sticky personal problem that could result in losing two people for the price of one. Others object that relatives may tend to waste excessive time together. All of these fears are groundless. In fact, a job recommendation by a staff member for a relative is not normally something given lightly. Often, relatives do not want to work together. How many wives enjoy working with their husbands? How many mothers would want to work with their daughters, or vice versa? Siblings view a common working relationship with equal caution because, with the love of an intense familial relationship, frequently there is some friction that makes constant companionship uncomfortable.

In fact, nepotism more commonly consists of hiring one's own relatives or the relatives of others for positions not accessible to the power of the boss. When one recommends (or suffers) the hiring of a relative in a close-knit organization, an element of risk is added to your own position. If the relative fails in the job it is bound to reflect poorly on the employee who already works in the company. Imagine the trauma caused by having a brother, sister, mother, daughter, or son fired. Staff fear such trauma in practice, and do not tend to recommend a relative unless they are extremely certain that the relative will succeed.

When job openings occur, give your staff ample opportunity to recommend their friends and relatives, and consider their recommendations without bias. When a relative fits the mold and is hired, orientation is normally easy and assimilation very rapid. There is an air of extra excitement over the hiring of a true family member, and a warm desire to meet and become acquainted with him.

Failures do occur from time to time, but both the organization and the remaining relative normally survive the difficulty. The saying goes, "it is far better to have loved and lost." Similarly, it is better to enjoy the benefits of nepotism in a business than suffer its arbitrary rejection because of unfounded fear of contrived problems.

We do not mean to say that nepotism is a must or that one should actively try to insert it into the orbital system. Very simply, where nepotism is encountered or when it can be introduced into the system as a benefit, don't be afraid to work with it, rather than avoiding the issue entirely.

Chapter 12 /

Making Work Fun

Mixing Business with Pleasure

MAKING WORK FUN may sound like a sophomoric objective, but through careful development of pleasing activities the sharp line between work and play can be turned into a smooth transition. All of us spend a majority of our productive waking hours at a job. To totally wall off that element of our life as dry, difficult, obstacle-laden activity gives a rough contrast to our lives that requires constant transition from family and leisure activities to work, and back again. It is far better for all of us emotionally to integrate work into our private lives and pleasure into our work lives—achieving a balanced quality of activity. In practice, most people do indeed achieve some such mix in their daily lives, but the orbital management system strives to maximize it.

It is the rare company that does not offer an employee picnic and tolerate if not sponsor a bowling or softball team. Less common, however, is the deliberate restructuring of the office social activities to ensure a bountiful measure of offerings which keep the staff buzzing wtih excitement and anticipation of the next event on the calendar. Such activities can be limitless, running the gamut from adventure outings (including whitewater rafting, canoeing, hiking, skiing, horseback riding and camping trips) to team ventures such as basketball, volleyball, or bowling. They can include more sedate functions—hayrides, picnics and theatre parties. Staff members enjoy organizing these activities in turns, and recruiting fellow employees to participate. Inevitably, some of this activity planning (and employee discussion of coming events) takes place during the work day and on company time, but this is generally minimal and generates a higher level of staff enthusiasm which carries over into each day's work. It adds to the positive electricity in the air of an orbital system company. The bottom line is increased, rather than decreased, productivity.

Forgive us if we sound idealistic. We are certainly not encouraging *high* levels of socialization. But people are social creatures and socialization takes place within any organization whether management allows it or not. With reasonable freedom to socialize, people create a work atmosphere where they are willing to work harder and longer than in an environment where the opposite is true. Any organization concerned about its employees should be seeking optimal productivity, not maximum productivity. With maximum production, an organization sacrifices quality in workmanship and creativity by employees. It creates an environment where employees punch in at 9:00 a.m. and cannot wait to punch out at 5:00 p.m. With optimal production, the goal should be towards excellence in workmanship and creativity. When one is allowed the freedom to socialize, to shape one's job, and to hold some autonomy, more effort tends to be applied towards organizational objectives. Don't forget that we are trying to motivate and instill pride in our employees—goals directly relevant to how the employee perceives the work environment. Socializing, autonomy, and job-shaping are all a part of that environment.

It is a fallacy when management believes that maximum productivity is a result of the total number of hours and minutes in the course of each day spent with staff noses to the grindstone. Productivity weighs significantly more heavily upon the efficiency with which work hours are utilized. Disgruntled employees of a mechanized insurance office may appear to have their noses to the grindstone every minute of the day not allocated to preassigned lunch and coffee breaks. In truth, poor efficiency results from low job satisfaction and eliminates job effectiveness. That fraction of time spent on the job which maximizes job satisfaction through work diversions results in a pittance of the loss experienced by dissatisfied employees who plod listlessly through their day.

One daily activity that ties in with this philosophy is no less mundane than lunch. The simplest yet most rapidly recurring activity to plan is lunch. Special potluck sharing among staff groups can heighten the enjoyment of each week's activity. Lunch can be a free-wheeling happening in the orbital system, where good will, good food and good fun create a healthy revitalization each day. Even when lunch is a gathering of brown-baggers in a meeting room, it provides a welcome release from workday tension. It can be a preplanned group lunch with individuals contributing ingredients to the super fruit salad, a taco party, a gourmet baked potato lunch, or whatever one's imagination can conjure up for culinary variety. Any one of these bring lunch time out of the ordinary to the level of clever, crazy or even gourmet. In any event, group lunches can be one of the simplest devices for mixing business with pleasure on the job while regenerating enthusiasm for the long afternoon home stretch of the day's effort.

Another informal company activity that literally helps to lift the spirit is the happy hour gathering at the local watering hole. TGIF[1] parties are always a hit but from time to time a midweek gathering can productively break up a work week as well. Only a bulletin board signup sheet is needed to tell the staff who might be interested in whiling away an hour or two after work before heading home. Parties like this will obviously attract more singles than married staff, but the greatest fun can come if spouses are persuaded to join the gatherings. It's informal, easy, and low key; it doesn't need much response but keeps everyone aware that an office that works together can play together as well.

This brings us squarely into the general subject of socializing with colleagues after work—whether they are "superiors" or "subordinates." Happily, if you enjoy your colleagues at work they may offer additional pleasure and companionship away from the job without the pitfalls inherent within a hierarchy. There is no confining social atmosphere in orbital management because there is no natural awareness of a hierarchical pecking order—all employees are basically equal except in pay and responsibility. There is definitely not an attitude of superiority or inferiority pervading any relationships in an orbit—attitudes which commonly make outside socialization in a hierarchy false and uncomfortable except among peers on equal management levels. Even promotions frequently disrupt prior social relationships in a hierarchy.

There are many reasonable objections to outside socialization with superiors or inferiors in a hierarchical system. A superior may feel uncertain of an inferior's friendship, perhaps interpreting it as buttering up the boss or currying favor with a superior. A superior must wonder if he can be a back-slapper at a weekend party and bark orders at the same person on Monday morning. He may wonder if promotions to rank or responsibility will be viewed as favoritism by co-workers who are not his close friends or, worse yet, if he can reprimand or ultimately fire a friend? These are very real problems even in the orbital management system where superior/inferior terms and relationships are happily moot. There are real downsides to the system which cannot be ignored or naively dismissed. They do happen. But historically these pitfalls are heavily outweighed by the daily feelings of good will and trust that permeate the orbital management system, where socializing within the orbit is not only tolerated but encouraged.

One must always pay a price for freedom. Just as America has paid a price for its freedom and democracy through a variety of public conflicts, there will be times in orbital management when total democracy is more complex and problematical than the more common autocratic bureaucracy. But few employees in the system would willingly sacrifice the continuous good will it generates in order to eliminate the rare acrimony that can develop when problems at work disrupt an earlier pleasant and fulfilling orbital social relationship.

So work together, party together, vacation together if you will, without concern for different levels of office responsibility, and let the chips fall where they may. Life is too short for a conservative position which limits the potential joys of human friendships. Those who wish to steer clear of such relationships may do so, while those with a devil-may-care attitude should exercise it. Such is the laissez-faire attitude of orbital management.

Orbital Atmosphere: A Reinforcing Environment

Warmth, openness, and good taste are important features to consider when orbital offices are laid out. It is foolish to be penny wise with investment in an atmosphere where employees spend the majority of their working hours trying to make a productive contribution to their own lives as well as to the company. While some workers toil oblivious to their surroundings, completely absorbed in and dedicated to the work, more by far are turned off or on by their surroundings.

An office environment needs to be planned with people in mind, not only to make the work flow efficiently, but to make people comfortable and happy to stay in that environment. The difference between a cold, sterile office and a warm, comfortable, beautiful and homey office is only a few pennies a day per employee, when amortized and depreciated over a ten-year period and divided by the number of employees in a company.

The office environment can and should be attractive enough to make people as "at home" at work as they are at home. It will pay off—people will not watch clocks, will not mind working late, or even on weekends. People will simply enjoy being at the office for the sake of being there, and that's part of the idea.

Special care should be taken not to establish a hierarchy of office decoration. All spaces should be equally nice though not necessarily equally as large. In fact, a case can be made for reverse hierarchical discrimination in office decoration. Those with the least responsible and often most monotonous jobs should have the most attractive offices, and certainly the best available view if it is possible.

An orbital organization should provide employees with a unique atmosphere. Office decor and motif play an important role in instilling that atmosphere. Even such amenities as weightlifting equipment, exercise rooms and outdoor running tracks or fitness centers add not only to the health of employees but also to their productivity. These amenities allow individuals to break up their day and promote longer working hours, and by using such material concepts of the orbital management office the true impact of the system can be brought home in no uncertain terms. Everyone is dealt with equally and thoughtfully, because the orbital system really cares about its employees.

NOTES

1. Thank God it's Friday.

Chapter 13 /

Loneliness and the Paymaster

WHILE OPENNESS, HONESTY AND DEMOCRATIC PRIN-CIPLES PREVAIL in the orbital management system, one sacred area of the management game must be played in secret. That area is employee salaries. A contrast in management freedom can be seen in a labor union or the federal government, where the hierarchy achieves its ultimate level of constraint and frustration in suffocating the lives of employees. Yet even in these rat-like maze operations, every job has a code number establishing the salary value. Everyone knows or can figure out what the next person earns. It may be a small point of freedom in a highly restricted system but it adds nothing to the satisfaction of the employee.

Frankly put, one's salary, like one's sex life, is no one else's damn business, except for the paymaster, other responsible bean counters, and the COO. As close as the orbital system may approach utopian levels of human satisfaction, remember that staff are still human; jealousy and avarice can still create frustration and dissatisfaction. Salaries are a *personal* statement of an individual's value to a company and should not be public knowledge. Discrepancies in salary between members of a hierarchy are firm, established, recognized, and accepted if not necessarily agreed with, but in the orbital system variations are more delicate and may not be as widely accepted if known.

Such discretion and acceptance is often more easily aimed for than attained. While there may be a few people who will bandy about their personal remuneration, either to brag or complain, it is not common and should be *discouraged*. The more normal leak in the system is a sloppy paymaster who secures neither his files nor his lips.

The best way to make salary figures secure is to employ a paymaster whose zeal for confidentiality rivals the religiosity of a fundamentalist preacher, but with a lower profile. When only one staff member carries the weight of knowledge about each employee's salary, he needs special personality characteristics to cope with peer pressures. In the orbital management system it is said that everyone is equal except on payday. This is an excellent concept which allows operation of a totally democratic organization with no pecking order. Mail clerks and department heads are treated with the same courtesy; they in turn, respect each other as equal "oar pullers" in the organization. Clearly, however, all staff will know that the level of responsibility carried by individuals in different positions varies significantly, and that financial remuneration is keyed to responsibility. Let us emphasize that *only the remuneration* (among all other trappings of position) should be variable. There will be no executive washrooms or dining rooms, no tiptoeing past a boss, nodding nervously. There should be no protocol[1] among employees except the everyday manners of the Golden Rule we all learn but often do not use.

The ability to keep salaries confidential rests largely with the paymaster who must take his position very seriously to maintain the confidence of the entire staff. All staff must be made to understand that salary is a subject for discussion only between an individual and the company officers who establish it. It is in everyone's best interest that salary information remain confidential; the burden of achieving this rests continually with the paymaster who will, from time to time, be cautiously asked to divulge some payroll inner secrets.

To resist pressure from friendly employees requires a dedicated person who takes the job seriously and who has the self-learned tact to turn people away but not off. A paymaster may have to establish a cloak of loneliness, a little distance that makes the goal more achievable, but his ability to carry off the role successfully will make the policy effective and respected in the company, to the benefit of the system and the individuals who work in it.[2]

NOTES

1. Though we stress no protocol, we realize this is easier said than done. Lehr, himself, tends to be a bit intimidating because of his position in the organization and the respect his employees have for him. He overcomes it with a self-effacing air, a devil-may-care attitude and an upbeat disposition.

2. We are not assuming or suggesting that one use a single employee to distribute salaries. This would counter all accounting principles. What we are suggesting is that salaries should not be made known to those who are not necessarily involved, i.e., anyone other than those who type, approve, sign and receive the paychecks.

Chapter 14 /
The Temporary Need for
Martial Law

EVEN IN THE HIGHLY DEVELOPED DEMOCRATIC SYS-
TEM OF ORBITAL MANAGEMENT, periodic episodes of crisis
may require the temporary relinquishment of social niceties in
favor of rapid-fire, military-style response. Martial law is a system
utilized in many societies to create a militaristic action-oriented
organization in time of civil strife. Democracy has clearly proven
to be the most wondrous of all forms of government when
measured in terms of human happiness, satisfaction and emotional fulfillment, but it is not an efficient management structure
when life-and-death-like decisions must be made quickly. Democracy in a sense is government by committee where many view-
points are heard before a decision is made. In a crisis, lag time in
decision making can spell doom for society. Today, too often, we
associate martial law with a takeover by a military group that
proclaims itself to be the new government in that country. Frequently, martial law is maintained long after an actual crisis has
passed, in order to assure the control of the military group who
do not wish to yield to a more popular form of leadership. The
term, therefore, has gained a very negative association in every
day life but has its place in every form of organized life, be it a
business or a government.

The orbital management system is based on an optimum level of democratic principles, but there are times when it must yield to a speedier, less democratic decision making process. It is then that the chief operating officer and often his department heads must assume dictatorial powers over the individuals with whom they normally integrate rather than supervise.

There are obvious situations where the need for this temporary hiatus in the orbital system occurs. In a production-oriented organization, it may come up when a deadline for a product is so close and production so far behind that the luxury of time for playing catch-up no longer exists. Temporary and rapid restructuring may be required to increase productivity for a brief period of time to reach a critical deadline and avoid long-term disasters for the company. It makes no difference if one is in production of printed material, mechanical equipment, insurance or carpet cleaning. We all know these situations arise. When they do, we must have the will and conviction to drop the usual warm and friendly interchange for the firmer direction of the military hierarchy. Apologies and the rekindling of the normal orbital social atmosphere can be left for a celebration at the conclusion of the crisis. If the staff has been forewarned when they first enter the orbital system and if they are periodically reminded that such crises can occur, this need never pose a problem. The well-briefed staff will understand that martial law may occasionally be used, but only when absolutely needed; few of them will be unable to make the short-term adjustment.

A longer-term period of marital law may be required if financial crisis strikes an organization. Faced with intangible red ink, a company will need to put on its horns, cut its fat, and get down to fighting weight in a series of cost-cutting moves probably unpopular within the free-wheeling orbital system. When push comes to shove, survival must be the overwhelming objective even when it is at the expense of individual employee happiness or fulfillment.

This sudden change in management style may be difficult for the chief operating officer to live with. He may hear from staff that "Life may be rosy, democratic and flexible when things go well but when the chips are down, the company is no different than any other." This comment will be absolutely true. When the chips are down, the militaristic hierarchical system (for short periods of time) is indeed more effective. It was developed for organizations where, for one reason or another, the chips are always down. Autocratic behavior has its place, but the orbital manager must be strong enough to bite the bullet from time to time, recognize when harmonious interface must give way to an alternative approach, and plan to restore the orbital status quo as soon as possible.

In a well-run company, martial law should rarely be needed. Clearly, a monthly occurrence would be an indication of serious problems in the conduct of business that consistently require a catch-up strategy. But all managers make mistakes, from time to time. Part of the price they must pay in the orbital system is the admission that there may be times that there will be temporary requirements for marital law.

The negative impact of martial law within the orbital system can be dramatically reduced if drills are held anticipating times of crisis. Somewhat like a fire drill, where every individual takes a new station in the company with speed and determination, martial law can be achieved quickly and efficiently in order to attain a short-term result. Debriefing programs at the conclusion of the crisis (whether it lasts a day, week or month) will help the staff to fully understand why the crisis occurred, why it needed to be handled in an authoritarian manner, and how return to orbital management and its associated social advantages can be implemented in an expeditious fashion.

Call it what you will, but some kind of martial law or structured system must be available in an orbital system for those situations where strict discipline must be used temporarily. The two most important things to remember about a martial law policy is that 1) it must be effective in achieving short-term goals in line with company objectives and 2) that it is temporary. Utilizing a martial law policy constantly or on a regular basis, or instilling the policy when it is not necessary, at worst constitutes an abuse of the policy and at best subverts the underlying premise on which an orbital system is based.

Chapter 15 /

Abuse

GIVEN ENOUGH ROPE, SOME PEOPLE WILL HANG THEMSELVES. Given enough freedom in the orbital system, some people will abuse it from time to time. Anyone in an orbital management system normally recognizes that its success hinges on the quality of its people. Some believe the system only works with exceptional people. We believe that most people can eventually be shaped into optimistic, motivated, self-starting employees who will thrive under orbital management. Let us repeat that hiring and orientation practices are crucial to the ultimate success of the system. We want to be with people who appear to have the emotional stability and independence that flourishes in our free-wheeling, creative environment. When employees join the staff, they must be shown how and where they fit and how wide the boundaries of their flexible niche actually are within the company. But none of us judge people perfectly—we can be fooled and conned by pleasant people, or we can make the mistake of placing too much confidence in individuals whose character does not merit trust.

Those individuals lacking appreciation for the broad realm in which to achieve see, instead, voids in their responsibilities which can be filled with inactivity and wasteful leisure. If not driven, they stand still. The orbit in which they revolve begins to break down, productivity suffers and, without strict routinization, job descriptions, or schedules of requirements, the problem may not be immediately obvious. But any weak link soon becomes clear to other people within the orbit. Initially, good natured criticism will come from co-workers and eventually, if improvement is not seen, criticism will work its way up to orbits of greater responsibility. The system will tend to preserve itself; abuses will not stay hidden for long.

If abuse is allowed to continue for a significant period of time, the democratic structure of the orbital system can begin to break down. Comments will be heard about employees who are breaking their backs to achieve for the company, while others sit around and vacation on company time. On the other hand, individuals well-seasoned in the system, who have historically seen what ultimately happens to abusers, will be more inclined to sit back and sympathize, knowing that slackers will be extricated from the system and not realize "how good they have had it, until it's gone."

Abuse in the orbital system must be investigated thoroughly and expeditiously. Managers must talk to the individual's co-workers at all levels of the system, realizing that everyone is really on the same level in this system. It is highly important to get the abuser's point of view on what appears to be an apparent lack of self-motivation and a disinclination to establish adequate personal productivity goals. As in all companies, warnings are the first line of defense and firing the second. The timeframe between warnings, continual dissatisfaction and firing should be short within the orbital system because so much depends on an atmosphere of equity and fairness for the entire staff. Toleration of abusers for a period that appears too long will create overall staff dissension and fray the system.

Strong interdependence among staff is not a controlling factor in a hierarchical system. Inadequate employees can therefore be tolerated for a longer period of time without badly upsetting the scheme of the organization.

Make no mistake, there will be abuse and there will be abusers. People are not perfect and no manager's judgment is perfect in choosing employees and nurturing their development. Just as new staff members should be apprised of the ways in which martial law is periodically implemented, they need to be told how abuse is handled. Abuse should be discussed in annual meetings. When staff members must be terminated for conduct deleterious to the system, the termination should be dealt with quite openly.

In a sense terminations require a brief moment of martial law when quick, decisive action is required on the part of the terminator. Abuse and abusers will surely creep in as night follows day, but the rate of occurrence will generally decline as managers gain more experience. Time will improve managerial judgment about how to select people initially who can work within the system, and it will concurrently improve the ability to see problems as they develop rather than after the problems have matured. This will provide the potential for long-range prevention or correction of problems before they have gone too far. On the other hand, frequent occurrences of abuse and the existence of abusers for long periods certainly indicates poor judgment on the part of those individuals responsible for hiring staff and managing them. Many situations can be greatly mitigated if periodic meetings are held where department heads and the chief operating officer review personnel strategies, trade problems and solutions and thereby prevent or correct problems by becoming forewarned. Do not be too concerned with abuse. It's a part of life and no management system is perfect. Just recognize that an orbital management system can approach perfection[1] at a much faster rate and on a closer path than the hierarchical system can.

Notes

1. Perfection in the business sense; that optimum level of efficiency.

Chapter 16 /

The Board of Directors . . . A Necessary Evil

BOARDS OF DIRECTORS HAVE LONG BEEN THE BUTT OF BUSINESS JOKES in modern day society—hiring and firing the COO may be their only saving grace. Boards are frequently seen as obstructional groups of good ole boys who stick their noses in management without adequate preparation or understanding of the timely problems facing a company. They tend to involve themselves in minutiae where they feel confident and ignore general policy directions where they are supposed to have more meaningful background, experience and presence.

Robert Townsend's book *Further Up The Organization*[1] humorously suggested that boards of directors should meet standing up, in board rooms, to shorten meetings to tolerable limits. This is probably unfair, because a well-chosen board with specialized background skills and experience can add wisdom and judgment that alleviates the common management problem of losing sight of the trees so often hidden by the forest. The board should logically have three primary functions. First, that of oversight. They need to ensure that a company attempting to follow a particular path is not missing significant opportunities in other directions. Second, the board should view overall productivity against the background of their own experience, as a gauge of the degree to which the company is fulfilling its potential. Finally, the board's only impact on the day-to-day management of the company should be its ability to judge the chief operating officer, and to terminate him if it appears to be in the best interest of the company. Short of that, no interference with management should ever be attempted. Though the average board of directors is too often a necessary evil required by corporate law, it need not be so. If directors are carefully selected for their skills, experience and ability to make unlimited contributions, rather than on the basis of friendship or other associated reasons, the board can be a true asset. Meetings should indeed be infrequent and short, with no time wasted in endless reports of good news. Background material to be studied by boards should be prepared with tremendous care to successfully summarize all the valuable information necessary to their task. The board should be fully apprised of the way an orbital management system works, to avoid surprise when members visit the company office and see the system operating in its free-wheeling fashion. When directors join orbital management companies, they must be made to recognize that parallels cannot be drawn from their own hierarchical management experience—they should not give free advice about the operation of an orbital management system. All of us who are orbital system managers should make every effort to sell the system to our boards of directors, if only for the personal satisfaction gained when awareness of a better working environment is expanded to include others.

A poorly chosen board can be truly hazardous to an orbital management system because board power can be used disruptively. Thus, choosing the board needs to be done with every bit as much ingenuity and sensitivity as the choosing of staff. Acclimate the board of directors to the orbital management environment and ensure continuity between the board and the company. If directors are trained to think with the normal positive attitude inherent in the democratic orbital management program, they may eventually become as creative and productive as the staff itself. When that occurs, the board is no longer a necessary evil but an attractive addition; members will make an independent contribution to the very creative process upon which the orbital system was developed.

It is important to remember that—whether a company is changing board members, acquiring key managers or just involved in the normal hiring of employees—the orbital management system must be preserved. During such crucial times there may be a tendency to revert to a hierarchical institution because an employee or executive may not assimilate properly with the orbital system or, in fact, may attempt to subvert the system. Remember that there is no such animal as an "indispensable employee." Any appropriately-paid individual within an organization can be replaced. Exceptions mean that either the individual is being taken advantage of, or that the organization is being "taken for a ride." To repeat an earlier theme, the object of an orbital company is not to make money off the backs of its employees but, rather, to have the employees make money for the organization. Assimilation of employees from the staff level and beyond to the board level is critical to the survival and perpetuation of the orbital system.

NOTES

1. Townsend, Robert. *Further Up The Organization*. New York: Alfred A. Knopf, Inc., 1984.

Chapter 17 /

Reflections of Company Image

SINCE ORGANIZATIONS TEND TO DEVELOP AN IMAGE of themselves which may be far removed from reality, periodic inspection and reflection is essential to minimize this erosive propensity. Almost nothing is worse than to purport to be what one is not; true for organizations as well as individuals. "You are what you say you are" may be a psychological anthem for some people who believe in the power of positive thinking, but the anthem doesn't work in business. Actions speak louder than words in business as in other aspects of life. An organization can call itself flexible, democratic, warm and compassionate and, in fact, be none of these things. Employees do not believe what they hear, they believe what they feel. Orbital management systems are dynamic and electric. The force can be felt within a very short time, not only by every staff member but, quite amazingly, by visitors moving within the system. Saying you have an orbital system doesn't make it so. Managers and units within companies may attempt to install orbital management systems but, if they hold back in all the places where change really counts, the result is just a hierarchical system by another name. A rose by another name will still be a rose; reform of the overbearing, disconcerting hierarchical system so many of us wish to escape requires more than a name change.

Many companies concentrate on public image. They go to great lengths to show consumers that they are environmentally aware and concerned with community and public relations. Most companies feel that this type of image will help to increase their sales levels and convey a "good neighbor" attitude to the public, and there is no doubt that this image is very important to the public, as well as the company itself. But what about the image employees hold about the company they work for? It is very important that a company strive to enhance its image among employees and instill a working environment such as an orbital system maintains. Given a good working environment and atmosphere, employees will strengthen the company's image. When a good image and feeling about the company pervades the staff, it will permeate through them to the public beyond the boundaries of the organization.

In crude terms, put your money where your mouth is. Put your people where you say they are. Give them a chance to shine independently. And don't pull back from this freedom at every point of concern about failure. Like the little boy who cried "wolf," if you say you are when you aren't once too often, there is little chance that you ever will be. The orbital management system takes consistent courage, and the conviction that people must have the opportunity to stand on their own merit, to venture forth, to make mistakes, and to get up and try again. The true feeling is not so much given as it is learned. Orbital management systems must use a mirror frequently, not as an exercise in vanity but as an exercise in reality. Is the company really what you hope it is or is the system only a figment of your imagination? The real mirror is found in the faces of the staff. What are they thinking about the system? Is it what you hope it to be or what they hope it will be? Is it working or is it failing? It is very easy to convince ourselves that all is well when top management is happy and the company is reasonably prosperous, but if the staff is, in fact, dissatisfied, it may be a precursor of hard times to come.

Lest we sound as though we were describing the disparity between management and unions, perish the thought. The reality we described occurs within every orbit of the system between different levels of orbits and different levels of responsibility. It must be checked and rechecked at every turn. If it is not, trouble can truly develop into internal dissatisfaction that can eat away and destroy the system beyond any hope of revitalization.

A chief operating officer must keep a close watch on the reflections from management and staff. He is the one most likely to be deluded into a false attitude which hides problems far too long. On the positive side, however, problems of internal strife become more rapidly apparent within the orbital management system than in the hierarchy. As the chief operating officer rotates within orbits of the management system, he can judge quite clearly if the system is working. The hierarchical system, on the other hand, requires resident supervision by staff to ferret out negative attitudes toward the system and its current operations. So take the measure of the orbital management system often. The staff will reflect company success. A mirror can indeed reflect what you want it to reflect, but it will only be through the fruits of your dedicated labor.

Chapter 18 /

A Close Brush with Theory

THE AUTHORS HAVE LABORED ON THE FRINGE OF MANAGEMENT THEORY for more than a decade and feel fortunate never to have been sucked into its vortex.

All scientific disciplines are complete with esoteric jargon, and management science is no exception. In fact, it may be one of the worst because it is an area of expertise so easy to enter. So many of us become managers, and a significant percentage of us then begin to believe we know what we are doing and become students of management theory in an effort to define or design our approach.

We believe a little management science goes a long way. It appears to balance out as ninety percent B.S. and ten percent C.S. (common sense), and much of the literature reads like Lewis Carroll's "Jabberwocky."

In spite of cynicism toward the artificial intellectualism of management theory, we feel we owe it to our readers to exhibit at least a close brush with it, lest our credibility as narrators of management systems technology be questioned and weaken the value of the work at hand. We therefore offer the following theoretical support for our own relatively innovative "orbital management" technique.

An obscure but brilliant report by Warman and Joiner entitled "Planning, Management and Accountability in Water Resource Management" offers a brief view of selected management systems. The report lays responsibility for the currently faddish management-by-objectives concept at the feet of Douglas McGregor.[1] The MBO concept as Warman and Joiner explain it

> began with an emphasis on interpersonal relations. Developments in the behavior sciences during the mid-1950's to mid-1960's, led to a shift away from management techniques developed to "force" output from "reluctant workers."[2]

McGregor drew on Maslow's theory of human psychology in *Toward a Psychology of Being*[3] where Maslow defined the highest order of need as "self-fulfillment" which concerns the individual's desire to be master of his fate, and become all that he is capable of becoming.

From this point of view, McGregor developed his X and Y theories which are outlined and compared by Massie and Douglas in their text *Managing*.[4]

Theory Y

1. The expenditure of physical and mental effort in work is as natural as play or rest.
2. External control and the threat of punishment are not the only means for bringing about effort toward organizational objectives. Man will exercise self-direction and self-control in the service to which he is committed.
3. The average human being learns not only to accept but to seek responsibility.
4. The human capacity of imagination, ingenuity, and creativity is widely distributed among individuals.
5. In modern industrial life the intellectual potentialities of the average human being are only partially utilized.

Theory X

1. People have an inherent dislike of work and will avoid it if they can.
2. Most people must be coerced, controlled, and directed to get them to contribute to the organization.
3. The average person prefers to be directed, does not like responsibility, generally has weak motivation, and wants security and stability.

Clearly Theory Y, drawing from Maslow, led to the development of MBO which Robert T. Wallace writing for *The Bureaucrat* described as:

> nothing more than a management style based upon the promise that line managers will tend to do a better job if they: (1) state the net results they expect to achieve over a given period of time; (2) periodically assess their progress toward the end results, and (3) institute corrective or alternative action as appropriate.[5]

Theory X sums up the widely accepted concept that led to the hierarchical system characterized by the traditional bureaucratic organization still prevalent today.

Quite obviously the orbital management system rests on the tacit assumption that Maslow's statement of needs and McGregor's Theory Y are accurate evaluations of the state of man. This idea is not without scientific support, as indicated by Likert,[6] who presented strong evidence that a closely supervised organization is less effective than one which encourages personal creativity and thus human development.

Finally, in this close brush with theory we will conclude (as Warman and Joiner did in their research) with a quote from a study entitled "Beyond Theory Y"[7] by Morse and Lorsch which originally appeared in the *Harvard Business Review*.

> There is not one best organizational approach; rather, the best approach depends on the nature of the work to be done. Enterprises with highly predictable tasks perform better with organizations characterized by the highly formalized procedures and management hierarchies of the classical approach. With highly uncertain tasks that require more extensive problem solving, on

the other hand, organizations that are less formalized and emphasize self-control and member participation in decision making are more effective. In essence, according to these newer studies, managers must design and develop organizations so that the organizational characteristics fit the nature of the task to be done.

Having allowed the reader to ponder this learned quotation, we will claim the final word by stipulating our mild disagreement. We do not believe over the long haul that *anything* functions better with an "organization characterized by highly formalized procedures and management hierarchies of the classical approach."[8] Innovative factory managers have proved that "less formalized organizations" can be more, not less productive and, if one cares for people as well as products, it is always worth the effort.

NOTES

1. McGregor, Douglas. *The Human Side of Enterprise*. New York: McGraw-Hill, 1960.

2. Warman and Joiner. "Planning, Management and Accountability in Water Resource Management." Auburn University: 1976.

3. Maslow, Abraham. *Toward a Psychology of Being*. Princeton: Van Nostrand, 1968.

4. Massie, Joseph L. and John Douglas. *Managing*. New Jersey: Prentice-Hall, 1973.

5. Wallace, Robert T. "A New Test for Management by Objectives." *The Bureaucrat,* II. (Winter 1974). pp. 362–367.

6. Likert, R. *The Human Organization: Its Management and Value*. New York: McGraw-Hill, 1967.

———. *New Patterns of Management*. New York: McGraw-Hill, 1961.

7. Morse, John J. and J. W. Lorsch. "Beyond Theory Y." *Harvard Business Review*. May/June 1970.

8. Except of course in the case of military organizations where it becomes a necessary evil.

Chapter 19 /

Critical Mass

What Size Glory

NO SYSTEM OF MANAGEMENT WILL BE OPTIMALLY EFFECTIVE for a wide range of corporate sizes. Orbital management is most effective within a distinctive range of staff sizes and, happily, a majority of companies fall within that range. In Chapter 1 the structural diagram on page four shows the chief operating officer, five departmental orbits each with divisional orbits, and divisional orbits with group orbits. While one cannot draw an absolutely hard and fast structural model indicating the proper number of people for each unit, one can come fairly close to making a good case for optimum unit sizes based on the ability of workers at various levels to coordinate the work of others while maintaining high individual levels of productivity. For instance, starting in the outer realms of the orbital system with the group manager, it is probably a good idea for groups to average three individuals—a group leader and two staff members. This is the lowest level of responsibility, and the group leader should not be asked to coordinate the work of too many people. Obviously a group could have one orbiting staff member or it could have three, but we make the case for one leader and two staff members as an optimum unit. As groups tend to get larger, opportunities for others to become group leaders should be opened up by attempting to divide the group into multiple groups where clear delineations in job tasks can be made. This of course will not always be possible.

For the sake of argument let's assume three individuals to be the ideal group unit. The next step up in responsibility is the orbit of the division manager. Here we recommend that a division manager be generally limited to coordinating three groups which, at the optimum level, gives him nine people to oversee (three of whom are group leaders and six of whom make up the staff of those groups). Thus we are recommending that the optimum size of a division be ten people.

Keep in mind that individuals within an orbital system are not differentiated by hierarchical power, but by their ability to take on responsibility and coordinate the work of others while retaining their own individual productivity. It is best to begin at a simple level without overloading people who may be new to responsibility and self-determination. Thus we start out with a group leader who coordinates two people and then move up to the division manager coordinating three group leaders who, in turn, each have six staff members. The next level is that of a department head; here we recommend that no department have more than five divisions rotating on its outer orbit. This gives the department head five division managers to coordinate and each of them, in turn, coordinates three group leaders. The overall staff orbiting around the department head will stabilize at fifty individuals if all the positions within the division orbits are filled. With three groups to each division and a division manager and five divisions in a department, the departmental unit totals fifty-one people.

Finally we recommend that the system not exceed seven departments. That means that the chief operating officer would have seven departments under his direct coordination. The seven department heads (with the chief operating officer) make up the executive management group. Seven full departments, each with fifty-one people plus the chief operating officer, would be a company of 358 individuals. It is unlikely that all slots would be filled at any given time; the number of individuals in an orbital organization probably will be below 358. But 358 is the number of individuals we believe to be compatible and functional for an orbital management system. That may seem to the reader to be a fairly large number of people and a sizable company. It is, but the orbital system will work with that many people because it emphasizes so many different responsibility units or orbits that disburse the coordinating function; more people are given an opportunity to control their destinies and assist others, while enjoying the flexibility of the orbital system.

One can obviously argue for a larger or a smaller optimum size.[1] The authors have not, however, arrived at the recommended numbers in an arbitrary fashion but rather through many years of management experience which identified the number of people for which different levels of managers can be effectively responsible. We also recognize that the span of management is determined by other variables than size: the number of profit centers, the skills and tasks of the employees, as well as the function and the objectives of the organization.

It should be obvious to anyone that the orbital system would work exceptionally well in a small advertising agency with a dozen people. In fact many, many small organizations with twenty or thirty people are operating an orbital system without even recognizing it. Hopefully this book describes in detail what is already happening in many firms.

Spinoff From Critical Mass

Two orbital systems under one corporate structure may prove superior to a single hierarchy. Let us outline here the arbitrary limits which tend to determine the size of an orbital system which can be effectively managed by a single chief operating officer and his department heads. We say arbitrary because, indeed, the whole concept is dependent to some extent on the managerial skills of each individual within the system. At each level of responsibility there are limits to the number of people who can be loosely directed. As a person works his way through the responsibility orbits, more and more people can become dependent upon him for assistance. The healthiest systems perhaps will be found to grow from small to large over a period of time. Thus, a company may begin with a handful of people, build to a few dozen and grow, ultimately, to an optimum-size system of over 300 people under the direction of a single chief operating officer. We are unwilling, however, to admit that a corporate structure ever needs to outgrow the orbital management system.

Today, many major companies find that decentralized, independently operating units can be run as separate companies under a COO without the need to reorganize into the old-fashioned and unsatisfactory hierarchical system. If a company becomes too large and the jurisdiction of the chief operating officer truly becomes stressed beyond individual human capacity, it is advisable to consider spinning off additional responsibilities before the critical mass is reached where an orbital management structure may begin to break down. Many chief operating officers tend to be unwilling to spin off independent units—they may see it as a threat to enlargement of control or power. This inclination must be guarded against at all costs.

On the surface it may seem foolish to say that no one can effectively manage a company of over 350 employees. After all, the Fortune 500 consists of numerous companies with thousands of employees, all of whom line up at some point below a president or chairman of the board who is the particular head of the corporate structure. But the head of General Motors (and similar companies) would be the first to admit that he does not have a firsthand, working knowledge of many of GM's divisions. He is fiscally responsible for the operating output of the divisions but not their day-to-day management. If they were honest, few top management people would claim to be able to fully interact on an effective level with more than a few hundred individuals. It is unwise, therefore, as a company grows to a critical mass (which may vary in accordance with the nature of the business) to attempt to hold it together as some unwieldy mass of manpower. Spinning off into autonomous operating divisions—each with its own chief operating officer—is the most logical and effective way of growing while dividing the company into units that maintain the advantages of the orbital management philosophy.

Of course, as at General Motors, someone has to be in charge. In a growing company, the chief operating officer of the first orbital management unit will commonly kick himself into the title of chairman of the board, president, or some other penultimate title which gives him final responsibility over two large orbital management systems. Another option would be to operate at the center, with a management committee of two or more orbital management COOs who elect a chairman to oversee management by committee at the center. This is a preferable approach because, if and when spinoff does occur beyond the critical mass, a COO with the solo responsibility of overseeing two or more orbital management systems may find himself with little to do as (by their very nature) orbital management systems do not require day-to-day overseeing or supervision. They do indeed require coordination, but this can be done intramurally among the COOs. Cohesive coordination should be the guiding light in the face of potential controversy at the board level. In this way a couple of thousand people could make up half a dozen major units, with a committee of COOs to determine the long-range direction of the company and to make those kinds of decisions that coordinate output and maximize productivity. This could be done while still maintaining an even-handed tight ship of management. The diagram on the following page illustrates a possible organizational structure which incorporates several orbital systems.

Normally management by committee would not be considered appropriate, effective or efficient, but the orbital management system flies in the face of this widely-accepted norm because it legislates against the crass objectives of power in the board room or the president's office. It works instead in favor of equality and friendship, without the petty jealousies which develop in the hierarchical system where corporate executives may climb the ladder over the bodies of individuals who were once their peers.

Here it is necessary and important to remember that the orbital management system is basically founded on the concept of non-supervision where each and every individual, no matter what their responsibility, spends the bulk of their time in personal productivity rather than in supervising the work of others. Such a philosophy leads to a no-nonsense approach to getting the job done without risking the ire of co-workers who desire more power and the consequent trappings of office. Orbital management systems depend on self-effacing individuals whose primary objective is the welfare of the company rather than that of their own individual nests.

As growth occurs, the COO should gauge, at specific instances, where critical mass may be reached for his capabilities. For some, it may be well below the number suggested as optimum in this chapter. For a very few others, the number may grow beyond what our own experience indicates. It is far less important to set these orbital limits than it is to know that you will recognize the effective limits as they grow nearer.

We admit that there are certain comforts in a hierarchical system. It tends to be constant in growth of objectives and directions. The personnel ladder can essentially continue up or down without reasonable natural limitations. The lack of firm answers about the limit of growth or size of the company can be viewed as a detraction from the ultimate benefits of orbital management systems. But while there are always drawbacks which may not be insignificant, they are a small price to pay for the overwhelming benefits of this humanistic management con-

*Figure II. Committee Management Diagram of Multiple
            Orbital Systems*

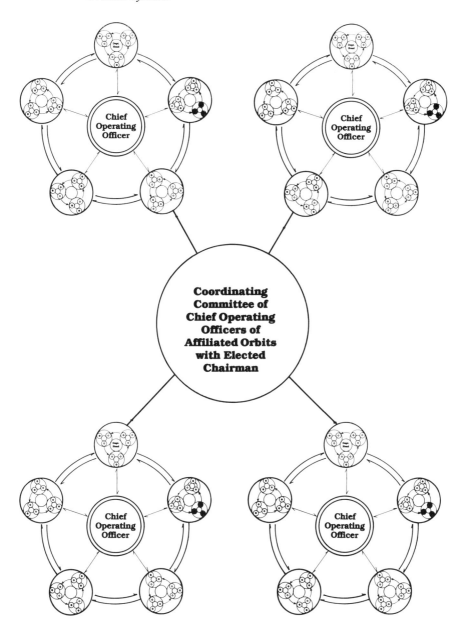

cept. We truthfully believe there are no limits to the size of the company that can be effectively managed with orbital management concepts.

NOTES

1. Orbital management systems can be larger with the structure of the organization only branched out further; that is to say that the units or groups are further from the center and the number of divisions increased.

Chapter 20 /

Orbital Management as a Solution

AN ORBITAL MANAGEMENT SYSTEM certainly is not a panacea for all organizational situations, but it provides a new approach for those organizations concerned with productivity, flexibility and employee relations. An orbital system does require a total commitment from management—this is a fundamental premise of the system's philosophy. From a well-established orbital system, one can expect a flat and decentralized management structure which is proactive rather than reactive to both its internal and external environments. Such a system incorporates a healthy and productive work environment which facilitates communication among different levels. The system is adaptable to many types of industries, particularly those dealing with uncertain tasks and problem solving functions as well as those involved with dynamic environments.

The orbital system is a humanistic management approach to organizational structures. It promotes self-management whether taught, created, or inherent within the individuals hired. As stated previously, it is not a system for everyone. But for those self-motivated individuals who need little supervision, an orbital system provides a haven for creativity, productivity and career molding. We believe that employees do not want to be managed; they would rather be led. If the proper environment is provided, self-management will indeed become the rule and not the exception. In this type of atmosphere, leadership will certainly prevail. What more could management want than an environment that leads to goal congruency while simultaneously satisfying both corporate and individual objectives and, at the same time, promoting the welfare of the employees? This would satisfy even the most finicky of shareholders.

Even if one does not agree totally with the orbital philosophy, instilling a partial system is clearly better than not adopting any orbital management principles. One could indeed develop an orbital system within a hierarchical structure among a division, department or profit center. It would be a difficult task but one well worth the effort. Many organizations already use some of the principles inherent in an orbital management system, through participative, Theory Y, or other humanistic managerial methodologies.

It is important to recognize that the orbital system is not simply just an organizational structure, but a living, organic system allowing change, creativity and flexibility. If a portion of an orbital system is destroyed, it simply regrows that particular orbit or set of orbits rather than destroying the entire system. Hierarchical structures can be so rigid at times that, with the destruction of an inherent element, the organization would literally march itself over a cliff. The real test of success for an orbital system is when a manager or key executive leaves the system. If the orbital system continues to grow and achieve the organizational goals consistent with orbital philosophy, then the system truly has integrated this innovative management concept. If it fails once a central individual leaves, then it is not a statement of the value of such an individual but rather the poor management technique exhibited by that individual and the remaining managers. The oribtal system can never survive if it depends on one person or even a few individuals. It survives on team work and the commitment by management to build a successful working environment.

Chapter 21 /

And Now For the Bad News

IT IS IMPORTANT TO BEGIN THE CONCLUSION OF THIS BOOK (on what we hope will be the future of business in America and abroad) with a penetrating analysis of all the negative criticism which can be realistically aimed at the innovative orbital system. Installing an orbital management system will never be easy—a vast majority of people will always oppose it as impractical, unreasonable and unworkable. Few have seen it done, few believe it can be done.

We have all grown up in a largely hierarchical society and tend to be pessimistic when it comes to management of the work environment. We do not really believe that work can be fun and still productive. We do not really believe that life can allow us to exercise the fullest range of our creativity and still contribute to the optimum productivity of a corporate structure. Those of us who do believe are often considered naive and out of touch with the realities of human nature. On every side, perceived realities legislate against the kind of corporate workplace that can and must be achieved if we are to move on beyond the hierarchical strangulation that has brought the industrial community to a point of sluggishness which threatens the successful growth of society. Most managers believe that most people require a watchdog in order to continue to produce at even a minimal level. Yet with watchdogs existing at every corner of business management today, we know full well that barely sixty percent of every forty-hour work week is spent in productive output. Management is strenuously seeking to increase productivity in every area of American business, yet the techniques we focus on are nearly always those of making machines produce more, rather than helping people to work more effectively.

Pound for pound we know full well that small businesses are by far more productive than big businesses. The reason, of course, is that each individual in a small company works harder for more hours than his counterpart in a large organization. Detractors will tell you that without constant supervision people will sit down on the job—this is often true, but true because the proper incentives do not exist within most hierarchical situations. It has been proven time and again that financial incentives have a limited impact on human productivity. Most people see themselves as earning a set amount of money; beyond that they do not appear willing to work for bigger and better things. The secret to productivity, however, lies within the human emotions of self satisfaction and personal fulfillment. Surely these are not easily achieved. This book has attempted in a precise manner to lay out the proper course to instituting successful orbital management systems. It has described without hesitation the many minefields planted along the way that can easily lead to failure in any effort. Tremendous faith in human nature is required. It is easy to give in to the doomsayers among us when the system does fall on its face from time to time.

Throughout most of the industrial age, the hierarchical system has been tried and has been found wanting. Today, more than ever, the limits to growth of our industrial society are seen clearly on the horizon. We must fashion a brave new world in business—a world that has the courage to ignore obstacles in the way, and climb over them one by one in an effort to make people and systems more rewarding. It is amusing to see the vogue for Japanese management in business today. Quality circles (and most of the other components of the fashionable Japanese management system) were developed in America in the industrial youth of this country and copied and operated more effectively overseas, while the business community of this country moved on to stricter, more dogmatic relationships that have left us all but stagnating.

People prove daily that there are truly no limits to man's capacity to attain greater heights of achievement, be it climbing a mountain or exceeding human physical endurance or penetrating the mind's capacity to understand the physics of the universe. The orbital management system simply states that similar limitations need no longer be tolerated within the working world.

Real education, understanding and empathy for human emotions hold the secret of success for orbital management. It is well known that human perseverance is far and away the greatest attribute for success. Formal education and human genius are useful but, in and of themselves, will never scale the heights. The world is replete with unfulfilled geniuses and educated derelicts. The orbital management system will lead human ability into the synergistic result of climbing one more mountain previously thought to be unreachable.

Orbital management is not for everyone and, once one recognizes those for whom it is not, they must be purged from the system or it will surely come apart at the seams. One needs the right people with the right attitude working in the right atmosphere toward high-minded objectives and reasonable goals to succeed, and succeed they will. It is said that good people are hard to find and that is true, but good people can be created— many more than the normal manager would ever believe to be true. And then again, does it really matter that orbital management may not be capable of taking over all of the business world? It only really matters that it can work for you.

Index

A

Absenteeism, 50–54
Abuse, 75–77
Advancement, 55–60
Anti-nepotism
  see Nepotism
Apple Computer, xv
Assistant to
  as title and negative descriptor, 45
Atmosphere
  of orbital system, 67–68
Automatons
  unsuccessful in orbital system, 10
Autonomy
  offered to orbital staff, 41
  see also Titles

B

"Beyond Theory Y," 86–87
Board of Directors
  role of, in orbital management; meetings, 26, 78–80

The Bureaucrat, 86–87
Burr, Donald, xv
Business with pleasure
  mixing, 64–67

C

Categorical organizations, 43
Company image, 81–83
CO_2, 5, 13
  sans secretary (advantages and disadvantages of), 46–49
COO
  as hub of orbital system, 5
Critical mass
  for successful orbital systems, 88–94
Cross-fertilization
  positive effects of, 11–12

D

Decision making
  orbital style of, 20–22
  participatory, 21

Democracy
abbrogation of, in crisis, 72
See also Martial Law
Departments
organizational position of, 4–5
staffing of; optimal orbital size, 89
Descriptors
avoiding negative, 43–46
Diagrams
Orbital Management Organizational Structure, 4
Committee Management Diagram of Multiple Orbital Systems, 93
Discipline
and maintenance of through orbital peer pressure, 9
Divisions, *see* Departments
Douglas, John, 85, 87

E

Education
value given to, and opportunities for, within the system, 57–60
Efficiency
versus creativity, 23–25
Equality
importance of systematic, 7–8

F

Flex-time
importance of in reducing absenteeism, and sick leave abuse, 50–51
Functional organizations, *see* Categorical Organizations

Further Up The Organization, 28, 47, 49, 78, 80

G

General Motors, 91
Gore, Inc.; and William Gore, xv
Groups, *see* Departments, Divisions

H

Hierarchy
defined, 1
Hiring, 10–11
of additional staff, 31
and evaluation of academic and experience credentials, 58
Hooky Day, 53–54
Hub
of orbital organization, *see* CO_2
The Human Organization: Its Management and Value, 87
The Human Side of Enterprise, 87

I

Indoctrination
creative, 24–25

J

Japanese management, xii, 59, 98
Job
creating your own, 35–38
see also Titles

L

Lateral movement, 38–40
Leadership
  planning for future, 6–7
Likert, R., 86–87
Lorsch, J.W., 86–87
Lunch time, 66

M

Management
  committee, 91–92
  roles, defining the, 14–16
  by objectives (MBO), 85–86
Managing, 85, 87
Martial law, 72–74
Maslow, Abraham, 85–87
Massie, Joseph L., 85–87
McGregor, Douglas, 85, 87
Meetings
  discussion and value of, 26–28
Mobility
  upward, 8–9
Morse, John J., 86–87

N

National Waterwell Association, xiii–xiv
Nepotism
  a new look at, 61–63
New Patterns of Management, 87

O

Office environment, 67–68
Officiousness, 46
Orbital management
  defined, 3

Orbital management system
  as a solution, 95–96
  criticisms of the, 97–98
  historical perspective on, 1–3
  introduction to, 1–13
  structural diagrams of the, 4, 93
Orbital travel
  inter- and intra, 38–40

P

Parsegian, Ara, 28
Planning
  in orbit, 17–19
  participatory, 19
Paymaster, the, 69–71
People Express Airlines, xv
Peter, Dr. Laurence J.; and
  The Peter Principle, 55, 60
"Planning, Management, and Accountability in Water Resource Management," 85, 87

Q

Queen Bee, 47–48

R

Retreats
  value of, 27

S

Salaries
  within the orbital system, 69–71

Screening
  of potential staff, 10–11
Secretary
  as title, 45
  and the CO_2, 46–49
Sick leave, *see* Absenteeism
Size, *see* Critical mass
Social activities and socialization, 64–67
Spaghetti syndrome, 30
Spinning off, *see* Critical mass
Staff
  breaking in new, 32–34
  deciding when to hire more, 29–32
  under-staffing, 29–30
Succession
  orbital, 7, 24
Supervision and supervisors, 11

T

TGIF parties, 66, 68

Theory
  a close brush with, 84–87
  Theory X, 86
  Theory Y, 85
Titles
  as identification of staff function, 41–46
  creating your own, 35–38
  see also Descriptors
Toward a Psychology of Being, 85, 87
Townsend, Robert, 26, 28, 47, 49, 78, 80

V

Volvo Corporation, 43

W

Wallace, Robert T., 86, 87
Warman and Joiner, 85, 87
Working day, the, 50–54